The Prayer of Saint Francis

LEONARDO BOFF

The Prayer of Saint Francis

A Message of Peace for the World Today

Translated by Phillip Berryman

ORBIS BOOKS
Maryknoll, New York 10545

The Catholic Foreign Mission Society of America (Maryknoll) recruits and trains people for overseas missionary service. Through Orbis Books, Maryknoll aims to foster the international dialogue that is essential to mission. The books published, however, reflect the opinions of their authors and are not meant to represent the official position of the society.

To obtain more information about Maryknoll and Orbis Books, please visit our website at www.maryknoll.org.

Library of Congress Cataloging-in-Publication Data

Boff, Leonardo.
[Oraçao de Sao Francisco. English]
The prayer of Saint Francis : a message of peace for the world today / Leonardo Boff; translated by Phillip Berryman.
p. cm.
Includes bibliographical references.
ISBN 1-57075-356-3 (pbk.)
1. Prayer of St. Francis of Assisi. I. Title.

BV284.P73 B65 2001
242'.7—dc21

00-051507

To the beloved Franciscan Province
of the Immaculate Conception in Southern Brazil
which initiated me in the tender dream
of Clare and Francis of Assisi
of brotherhood and sisterhood

PRAYER FOR PEACE
OF SAINT FRANCIS OF ASSISI

Lord, make me an instrument of your peace.
Where there is hatred, let me sow love,
where there is injury, pardon,
where there is discord, union,
where there is doubt, faith,
where there is error, truth,
where there is despair, hope,
where there is sadness, joy,
where there is darkness, light.
O Divine Master,
grant that I may not so much seek to be consoled
as to console;
to be understood, as to understand;
to be loved, as to love;
for it is in giving that we receive,
it is in pardoning that we are pardoned,
and it is in dying that we are born to eternal life.

Contents

Saint Francis
Still Living in Our Midst

Saint Francis of Assisi (1181–1226) is revered around the world as one of the figures who justifies pride in our humanity. His life story makes visible and possible dreams that we have carried all our life and cherish deep in our heart: a relationship of loving tenderness with God, our Father and Mother of infinite kindness; a simple love for all things, experienced as brothers and sisters; a gentle reconciliation between the impulses of the heart and the demands of thought; a warm welcome of strangers become neighbors, and of neighbors become brothers and sisters; a joyous acceptance of what we cannot change; an innocent freedom toward established orders and rules; a joyful acceptance of death as friend of life.

Saint Francis flooded the human realm with the spirit of good will, tender kinship, and peace, and that spirit has continued to reverberate through the years down to our own time. Churches, cities, schools, rivers, institutions, and people bear the name of Saint Francis (San Francisco) or simply Francis, in his honor.

Indeed, there are behaviors, symbols, ideas, and dreams that point naturally to Saint Francis as though he were their author. That is not surprising, because he continues to live as an archetype in the minds and hearts of people and of many cultural movements, in the spirit of nonviolence, universal kinship, joyfulness, love for animals, and ecology, all of which are important expressions of the spiritual searching of the culture of our age.

A diffuse Franciscan spirituality permeates our time, born out of the experience of Francis, Clare, and their early companions. This is the path of simplicity, of discovering God in nature, of simple love for all creatures, of almost childlike trust in the goodness of persons and in imperturbable joy, even in the face of the most poignant dramas of human life.

The Prayer for Peace, also called the Prayer of Saint Francis, has been an embodiment of this diffuse spirituality. It was not penned by the Francis of history, but it does come from the spirituality of the Saint Francis of faith. He is its spiritual father and hence its author in the deepest and most comprehensive meaning of the word. Certainly, without him, this Prayer for Peace would never have been formulated or spread. Much less would it have become one of the most ecumenical prayers existing today. Members of all faiths pray it, as do adherents of all spiritual paths.

It can bring everyone together in one spirit of peace and love. It can give us—even if only for a moment—the sensation that we are all really brothers and sisters in the great human and cosmic family, indeed sons and daughters of the divine family.

We are going to delve more deeply into the meaning of this Prayer for Peace so as to discover its unsuspected wealth and be able to awaken the Francis and Clare dormant within each of us.

How the Prayer of Saint Francis Came About

Great things often have humble origins. The Amazon, the most voluminous river on earth, starts in an insignificant spring between two fifteen-thousand-foot mountains south of Cuzco in Peru. The São Francisco River, the river that unites us Brazilians, starts in a tiny spring in the heights of the Canastra range in Minas Gerais. Slowly the waters join other waters until they form mighty rivers that empty into the vast sea.

Something similar has happened with the Prayer for Peace. It arose anonymously, out in the periphery, without anyone giving it any particular importance. Soon its beautiful and inspiring content was warming people's hearts and setting their minds on fire. Like a ray of light traveling through endless space, the Prayer for Peace kept spreading and winning over the world.

Everything in it is true and persuasive. It is so simple that anyone can understand it. It is recited by Buddhist children in Japan, Tibetan monks in India, Muslims in Cairo, Christian popes in Rome, base-community members in Latin America, and even workers in demonstrations and strikes. They all feel that this prayer is a very inspired translation of humankind's age-old desires. It connects with calls for peace and tolerance, which are absolutely necessary for our current perilous crossing from the local to the global, from the national to the planetary, from many societies to a single world society.

When prayers that are so inspired and universal emerge, it is a sign that their author is the Holy Spirit, who tends to act anonymously in the gentleness of hearts open to the divine. That must have been how the Spirit was at work in the unknown author who, full of spiritual fervor, gave shape to the prayer subsequently attributed to Saint Francis of Assisi.

The Prayer for Peace first appeared in 1913 in a small local magazine in Normandy, France. It was unsigned, and had been copied from another magazine that was so insignificant that it left no sign in history, for it has not been found in any archive in France.

From Periphery to Center

The Prayer of Saint Francis became widely known after it appeared in *Osservatore Romano*, the official Vatican newspaper, on January 20, 1916. The well-known French daily *La Croix* published it on January 28, at practically the midpoint of World War I (1914–1918), when prayers for peace were being offered everywhere.

How did the Prayer for Peace, or Prayer of Saint Francis, reach the Vatican, and then begin to spread throughout the world?

In dioceses and parishes throughout Christendom, people were praying for an end to the war that was bringing devastation and shame to Europe, the cradle of so-called Western Christian civilization. The Marquis de la Rochetulon, founder of the Catholic weekly *Souvenir Normand*, sent Pope Benedict XV several prayers for peace. It is not known whether the Marquis himself had written them or collected them from those circulating among the people.

That these prayers reached the pope is known because we have the note from Cardinal Gasparri thanking the Marquis de la Rochetulon on behalf of Benedict XV. That document reveals something interesting: all the prayers, including this one of Saint Francis, were directed to the Sacred Heart of Jesus, a devotion introduced to the whole church in the late nineteenth century.

The devotion to the Sacred Heart of Jesus sought to rescue a dimension forgotten in traditional Christianity: the richness of the sacred humanity of Jesus, his unconditional love, his mercy, his tenderness toward all, especially the poor and sinners, children and women.

As a result of this devotion, almost all Catholic churches around the world, even the oldest gothic, colonial, and baroque churches, have a statue of the Sacred Heart of Jesus with his heart plainly bleeding.

Devotion to the Sacred Heart of Jesus is connected with a humanitarian spirit of peace and reconciliation, something that was very much needed at that moment of world war. This was the context in which the Prayer for Peace was published in *Osservatore Romano*. Since then it has won the minds and hearts of millions of people around the world, and has been ecumenically transformed into a prayer for union among religions, which pray for peace, world peace, social peace, ecological peace, and personal peace.

Everything in it is simple and true, everything comes from the heart and goes to the heart. Anyone can respond to it by saying "Amen" and "Let it be so" with no confessional reservations.

From Prayer for Peace to Prayer of Saint Francis

How did this Prayer for Peace come to be called the "Prayer of Saint Francis"?

By a simple historical coincidence which is nevertheless meaningful and revealing. For there is a surprising affinity between the characteristics of the Heart of Jesus and those of Saint Francis. There is a reason why Saint Francis is called "the First One after the Unique One," or *Alter Christus,* other Christ.

Shortly after the Prayer for Peace was published in Rome, a Franciscan, a Visitor of the Lay Third Order in Rheims in France, had a poster printed with the figure of Saint Francis holding in one hand the rule of the Lay Third Order and in the other the Prayer for Peace with a reference to its source (*Souvenir Normand*). At the end was a short sentence: "This prayer sums up Franciscan ideals and also represents a response to the urgent needs of our age." With this short sentence, the way was opened for the prayer to be not simply a prayer for peace but also to become known as the "Prayer of Saint Francis," or the "Prayer for Peace of Saint Francis."

This prayer thus became a summation of devotion to the Sacred Heart of Jesus and of Franciscan spirituality. Curiously, the prayer of consecration to the Sacred Heart of Jesus published by Leo XIII in 1899 has a structure similar to that of the Prayer of Saint Francis we now have, especially the expressions in threes: discord-union, error-truth, darkness-light.

The other contrasting pairs—love-hatred, injury-pardon, doubt-faith, despair-hope, and sadness-joy—are anchored in the preaching of Jesus and in his liberating practice. His presence and word transform reality: where there is hatred, love comes forth; where there is injury, pardon appears; where there is doubt, faith emerges; where there is despair, hope is born; and where there is sadness, joy breaks out.

The second part, "Grant that I may not so much seek to be consoled as to console; to be understood as to understand; to be loved, as to love," constitutes a fundamental feature of Christianity, complete abnegation of oneself and of that which is dearest to us in order to be able to radically serve the other.

The third part, "For it is in giving that we receive, it is in pardoning that we are pardoned, and it is in dying that we are born to eternal life," is likewise grounded in the texts of the gospel:

- give and it will be given to you (Lk 6:38)

- forgive, and you will be forgiven (Lk 6:37)

- whoever seeks to preserve his or her life will lose it, and whoever loses it will keep it (Lk 17:33)

- whoever loves his or her life will end up losing it, but whoever hates his or her life in this world will keep it for eternal life (Jn 12:25).

Hence, the great kinship between devotion to the Sacred Heart of Jesus and devotion to Saint Francis has made it possible for the characteristics of one to be attributed to the other. This calls to mind the well-known expression of Father Antonio Vieira in his sermon on the Wounds of Saint Francis: "Clothe Christ and you will have Francis, strip Francis and you will have Christ."

This affinity appears, for example, in the writings of Saint Francis called the Admonitions, particularly number 27, where we find an obvious echo of the Prayer for Peace:

Where there is patience and humility
    there is neither anger nor disturbance.

Where there is poverty with joy
    there is neither covetousness nor avarice.
Where there is inner peace and meditation
    there is neither anxiousness nor dissipation.
Where there is fear of the Lord to guard the house,
    there the enemy cannot gain entry.
Where there is mercy and discernment
    there is neither excess nor hardness of heart.

It also appears in the prayer of one of Saint Francis's most mystical and profound disciples, Saint Egidio of Assisi:

If you love, you will be loved;
If you revere, you will be revered;
If you serve, you will be served;
If you treat others well, you will be treated well.
Therefore,
Blessed is he who loves without being loved,
Blessed is he who reveres without being revered,
Blessed is he who serves without being served,
Blessed is he who treats everyone well and yet is
    not treated well.

What is expressed here is the power of unconditional love. It loves for the sake of loving, without expecting any reward. This is the love that God has toward his sons and daughters, even when they are ungrateful and evil. This is the love of the Sacred Heart of Jesus. This is the love that

shone forth in Saint Francis. This is the love that con-
sumes mystics like Saint John of the Cross or the Sufi
Rumi. This is the love that brings any person eternal salvation, provides the basis for peace, redeems the world,
and constitutes the hidden meaning of the universe.

✠

Lord,
make me an instrument
of your peace...

Lord!

The Prayer of Saint Francis begins with an invocation, a true supplication: Lord!

"Lord"—*Senhor* in Portuguese—is a title of respect that we give to persons, especially those who are older or endowed with some kind of authority. "Lord" is also the most common name in most religions to express reverence for the originating Fount of all being, God.

The Bible translates the Hebrew term for God, "Yahweh," with the Greek word *Kyrios*, which means Lord. It appears almost a thousand times in the Judaeo-Christian scriptures. "Lord" was one of the first titles given to Jesus. Initially, it was used to express the respect of the people and the disciples for his word, his miracles, and his practice of liberating the poor and the oppressed. Later, after his resurrection, it served to emphasize his divine character as Son of God and his importance for our understanding of the final destiny of human beings and the world.

Applied to God, Lord means Creator of Heaven and Earth, because he has drawn all things from nothing so that they may be expressions of his superabundance of life and love. Because he is Creator, God is always present in everything, at the heart of all that is. If somehow God's creative will were to be suspended for a fleeting instant, all beings would revert to nothingness.

"Lord" also has a political connotation. The kings and those who dominate peoples make others call them "Lord," observes Jesus (Lk 22:25). The Roman emperors wanted to be called "Lord" to express their divine pretensions.

The first Christians reserved the title of "Lord" for Jesus and for God. They denied it to Roman emperors, and hence they were persecuted, brought before the courts, to the arenas, and to martyrdom.

The situation is not so different today. Powerful people in politics and finance present themselves as great lords. They meet among themselves to decide on the fate of millions of people. They demand total submission to their political, economic, and military strategies. Those in opposition are marginalized, excluded, and if necessary, attacked militarily.

There is a struggle among the various lords of the world to see which of them is most lordly. Nevertheless, religious people of all creeds deny the title "Lord" to these pretentious fools. In the name of the true Lord of Heaven and Earth, they unmask them as false lords, because their power is built up at the cost of the impoverishment of vast numbers of people and the systematic pillaging of the resources of the Earth. From a global standpoint, they are producers of death, rather than life.

In pronouncing this prayer and saying "Lord" to our-selves, we seek to recognize God as the true and only lord of history and human destiny. We pray that he may mani-fest himself as that creative Energy that enlivens all our energies of resistance and liberation, and do justice for the poor by reestablishing his lordship over creation, which has been entrusted to all humans as their heritage.

Today, because of the threats looming over the Earth and over humankind, and because peace and love are lacking on all sides, we not only ask, but we beg, crying out: Lord, Lord, hear us!

It was Jesus who taught us to insist even to the point of pestering (Lk 11:5-8). He will give us his peace, a peace achieved through service rather than through power. The Jesus of history accepted the title of "Master and Lord" (Jn 13:12), but changed its meaning. He became the servant of all because he understood his own existence as an exis-tence on behalf of others (Lk 22:27). He washed the disci-ples' feet and gave them a commandment to do the same.

The great spiritual masters like the Buddha, Moses, Christ, Krishna, and others were held to be "lords" by their disciples and by the multitudes. Even so, they regarded themselves as simple servants of God and of every human creature. This attitude of service, which breaks down barri-ers and encompasses everyone, brought with it peace, that true peace for which we all yearn.

Oh God, you are the only Lord of our life, our heart, and our destiny. Free us from the false lords that deceive us with their promises, for they bring neither life nor peace. Give us strength to resist and to seek peace through justice and the humble service of all. Amen.

Why no peace?

We pray the Prayer of Saint Francis for Peace because we need peace. Our times are agitated and violent and threaten the future of humankind and our shared home, the Earth.

Jesus has taught us, "Ask and you shall receive" (Mt 7:7). And so we ask insistently. And we want our prayer to be heard and to be efficacious.

What are our chances of having peace? We need to know what we can hope from our own strength and what we ought to entrust to God's strength. God and human beings never act separately. God has no other arms but ours. However, it is well to distinguish human and divine peace—so as to unite them immediately. The prayer itself suggests it: "Lord, make me an instrument of *your* peace." What is your peace and what is our peace? What is God's peace? What is human peace? True peace is attained only if both, human and divine peace, are connected and mirror one another. Otherwise our Prayer for Peace remains more word and song than communication and action.

For the sake of better understanding, we are going to examine the mechanisms of violence and the logic of peace. Meditating attentively on the Prayer of Saint Francis we discover in it the most persistent dramas and human hopes in history. Underneath its phrases is hidden something fundamental that has to do with the universe, life, and human history: their complexity, their contradictions, their possibilities.

We human beings feel ourselves to be the arena where contradictions break forth in a conscious and often dramatic way. When the drama becomes almost unbearable we cry out to our Father in heaven and we pray to our divine Mother.

Just as Jesus presented a summary of his message in the form of a prayer—the Our Father—so the complex and dramatic quality of reality is best expressed by a prayer, the Prayer of Saint Francis, or the Prayer for Peace. In it the depths encounter the mountain peaks and, spanning the whole, the rainbow of perpetual Peace embraces everything in cosmic communion.

The Shadows and Lights of Reality

How are things put together? They are full of chiaroscuro, lights and shadows, organization and disorganization, chaos and cosmos. Within the scientific community there is a broad consensus that we all came into being fifteen billion years ago out of an immense chaos, an unfathomable explosion. Its echo can be picked up by scientific devices even today. We have come from the cosmos, that is, from the order that was being created and is continuing to be created over billions of years. Chaos and cosmos are inseparable and interconnected.

No matter where we move or look, we find this same chiaroscuro, this same polarization: in the universe, in the vegetable world, in the animal kingdom. But it is especially in the human world that this complex reality unfolds its contradictions and gives rise on the one hand to murder, ecocide, and biocide, and on the other to guardian angels, prophets, and saints.

This wrenching situation is structural in nature: it is found in the structure of all beings, all undertakings, all institutions, and in the depths of each person's heart. There is no oasis of reconciliation or garden hideaway of sheer unity and unification. Everything is shattered. We must always begin anew, and again pick up the fragments to try to reassemble the precious vase in an untiring search for the one, the complex, the open, the fruitful, the relational.

The challenge lies in combining chaos and cosmos creatively, in drawing energies from both poles so that they complete us, and make us grow, and do not harm or destroy us. The Prayer for Peace highlights one pole, that of love, forgiveness, union, faith, truth, hope, joy, and light. If we focus solely on this pole, and if we pay no attention to the other which is also present, we will hold onto hatred, offense, discord, doubt, error, despair, sadness, and darkness. Directing ourselves to and strengthening the positive pole does not mean that we have canceled out the negative pole. But we can set limits to its harmful action, as the great spiritual masters of humankind have taught us. Jesus himself in his gospel reminds us that the tares and wheat are always mixed and there is no way to separate them for good. If we were to try, we would run the risk of pulling up the wheat with the weeds. What we can do is distinguish them and take an approach to life that is guided by the wheat without ever losing sight of the threatening presence of tares.

Spiritual masters and sages of all cultures are convinced that peace between persons and peoples is a matter of the soul and the heart. Those who wish to be on good terms with others—whether a people, a nation, a person, a social movement—must be on good terms with themselves. They must pacify their souls, become centered, and bring together the dispersing and scattering tendencies that conspire against peace.

Can we perform this task alone? No! Those same masters testify that, while we can do much by ourselves and are responsible for doing everything we can, that is still not enough. Hence we must open ourselves to the primordial Fount of life from which all peace emanates. If we do not drink from this Fount through prayer and meditation, our peace will be only a momentary truce, but never the peace for which our heart yearns.

As Saint Augustine continually reminds us, "Our hearts are restless until they rest in You, O Lord."

The Political Function of Religion

What has just been said applies particularly to politics, which is now integrated on a world scale. Politics operates on the old adage, "If you want peace, prepare for war." It is dominated by a self-interested and reductionist realism in the sense that it is organized around the interests of the most powerful rather than of all peoples and all human beings.

What is worse, political leaders, children of the modern state, have left the religious dimension out of their analysis of reality. They disqualify it as a residue of the irrational past of humankind or as a jumble of creeds, stories, and myths that are more of a hindrance than a help in the search for peace. Political leaders do not see that the secret soul of each people and each culture is in their religion, as so many anthropologists have attested. It is not in ideologies or isolated ethical principles, but in religion that most people find direction, illumination for their lives, and meaning for their suffering and their death.

Deep down, what is the glue that holds a society together? Is it not the deep convictions, basic attitudes, and traditions shared in common? And what ought to connect

and re-connect [re-ligar] all these factors, bringing about
sociability, relative harmony, and ways of keeping conflicts
under control if not the re-ligions? The mission of a religion or of a spiritual path is to keep alive the sacred memory of the central axis binding and re-connecting [re-liga]
everything; it is to reinforce the perception that things are
not thrown together randomly, but that everything is interconnected, everything forms a whole and participates
in one cosmic, earthly, and human history; and finally, it is
to give a name to the Fount of being and meaning, origin
of all, from which everything springs and toward which
everything is journeying, whether it be called by a thousand names or simply God.

There are good reasons why serious political thinkers
criticize the lack of attention paid to the religious factor,
which is decisive in the lives of people. They regret that
religion is "the forgotten dimension in state strategies."

As Hans Küng, one of the Catholic theologians who
has contributed most to a world ethic and to peace between religions, the basis for peace between peoples, has
correctly observed, "An analysis of the situation that
leaves out the religious dimension, no matter how scientific it may claim to be, is still flawed."

Disregard for the religious and spiritual factor also
closes off a priceless source of tolerance, human concern,
and peace, which is absolutely necessary for peoples, for
the environment, and for Mother Earth.

Roots of the Lack of Peace

Having laid the groundwork with these preliminary observations, let us now take up the central question underlying the Prayer of Saint Francis: why do we not have peace?

This question cannot be answered in terms of speculative reason alone. What we will present here is merely a groping attempt to plumb a mystery before which noble silence would be more fitting than profound thinking and saying a great deal. Yet reason, especially if made fruitful by faith, can lift up the veil over many depths and find reasons for silent contemplation.

Let us look now at three theories that attempt to account—albeit inadequately—for our lack of peace.

Lack of Peace: Rivalry and Envy

This theory was elaborated by the noted contemporary French thinker René Girard. According to Girard, the basic drive of human life is to be found in the structure of desire. Desire colors every dimension of our inner self and has an insatiable character. No matter how much we long for, focus in on, and conquer the objects of our desire, that drive remains ever unsatisfied and open to the infinite. Hence, desire is inexhaustible and gives rise to anxiety, unrest, and the sensation of a lack of peace. If people are unable to achieve their desires, they feel unhappy and exiled from the realm of serene and calm peace.

What can satisfy desire? What is the best way of desiring? In trying to answer these questions, human beings learn early on to deal with their desire by imitating others and desiring what others also desire. This tendency toward imitation serves as the basis for Girard's theory of "mimetic desire" (*mimesis* in Greek means "imitation"). Mimetic desire shapes our capacity for desire. Children express this plainly and transparently. Not content with their own playthings, they always desire what another child is holding. And they cry and become violent in the struggle to possess the desired object.

The anxiety to imitate results in the emergence of rivals who engage in a fundamental conflict. Two or more persons desire the same object; they enter into rivalry. Each seeks to eliminate competitors so that he or she alone may possess the object desired. But possession is not serene, because others will then imitate this person and again fight over the object. A chain of unending violence is unleashed. How can this destructive process be stopped?

One mechanism created by human beings was the introduction of the scapegoat, which took the place of all those who killed in order to possess the desired object. Instead of everyone else dying, the scapegoat died in their place. Its function was to enable everyone to unload their frustrated mimetic angers and desires. The scapegoat became the pacifying symbol, the absolute victim on whom the crimes of all were concentrated.

A rite of sacrificing the scapegoat was created (initially a person, someone innocent, a slave, a child, and subsequently an animal) through which all were reconciled. No longer did many have to die or kill because of the conflict produced by mimetic desire. The scapegoat died for all, in place of all. Now peace could take hold.

Cultures later replaced the scapegoat with laws and legal institutions, established orders and social institutions, which operate as a way of setting limits to human aggressiveness and ensuring that society operates peacefully.

But has peace been attained? The problem has simply been shifted, because it is painfully clear that all orders produce victims and leave people out. Within themselves they hide a camouflaged violence: those who do not fit into them are punished or excluded.

No known social formations or institutions, even those that are most universal, manage to include everyone. To maintain their identity, protect a particular order, espouse certain teachings or dogmas, and guard against caprice, they set forth minimum standards that have to be observed under pain of punishment or exclusion. For there will always be those who violate these standards or who withdraw from them for some reason, in the name of freedom or of some better order. And they will be punished or excluded.

Control, repression, and violence are reintroduced. The lack of peace becomes evident. Mechanisms for relieving guilt are created. New scapegoats are invented.

Every order (institution, church, political system, and the like) creates its "scapegoats": Jews for Nazism, communists for capitalism, members of the bourgeoisie for communism, subversives for military dictatorships, heretics for the Catholic Church, and so forth.

For the ideologists of capitalism, socialism served for fifty years as the great scapegoat, the anti-Christ. Its downfall was expected to result in a world of peace. What a laughable illusion! The result has actually been a new world order that is every bit as efficient at creating victims, because it is based on the world market whose cool logic is competition rather than cooperation. Two-thirds of all human beings are excluded from the benefits of development, victims on the altar of the Mammon of speculative financing. There is no peace in the work world, in companies, in national and world-scale politics. Violence reemerges in the shape of social exclusion, fundamentalism, and nationalism.

Everyone keeps living under the illusion that by eliminating the scapegoat the way to peace is finally open. But when one scapegoat is sacrificed, another is created. And so it goes. Human beings remain without peace, mistakenly seeking it on roads that lead to cul-de-sacs. They die of thirst before reaching the spring. Why? Because they do not succeed in creating societies where all have a place and do not need violence to maintain themselves, and so they create ever more victims and fail to achieve peace.

A great conversion becomes urgently necessary: rather than the mimetic desire that excludes, what must be brought in is the mimetic desire that includes and extends to the community the object desired. That way, all can share and benefit from it.

Why doesn't this inclusive strategy which brings about peace prevail? Why does negative mimetic desire predominate? Intellectual inquiry does not provide an answer.

Lack of Peace: The Mismatch between Consciousness and Death

This theory regarding the lack of peace in the human heart, and in interpersonal and social relations, comes from the modern psychoanalytic tradition.

In this view, there is in the human being an ongoing confrontation between two clashing forces: *eros*, which seeks life, and *thanatos*, which brings death. No matter how much one seeks to live, *eros* succumbs to *thanatos*. That is why it is so heard to accept death. This mismatch between life and death causes fear, the fear that death can enter in a thousand ways and complete its destructive work. And fear in turn generates violence, violence against everything that can threaten life or reinforce death. There ensues a state of permanent and extensive war and the foundations of peace disappear.

Here lies the origin of aggression: the fear that the other may threaten, take away, or diminish our chance of life. The other may be the bearer of the death that we reject, and hence is our enemy, who must be fought and eliminated under the illusion that our death can thereby be avoided. In the capitalist illusion of private and unlimited enrichment, the accumulation of power and wealth is sought as a desperate attempt to guarantee life over death. But death follows its inexorable course, and its scythe cuts down everyone without exception. Death triumphs over fearful consciousness, putting peace out of reach.

How to overcome this impasse, which is similar to the one found in the previous theory? Above all, the category of "enemy" must be abolished. How to do that? By casting out fear, which produces violence. Fear is driven away when trust, unconditional love, and especially care enter the scene. When human beings start caring for one another— caring for the common good, health, education, housing, free communication, the environment—then the causes of fear disappear, because no one is threatening anyone.

This is the lesson of all spiritual masters and wise politicians. It is the lesson left to us by Jesus. He spoke of unlimited love for neighbor. They asked him: Who is my neighbor? Rather than giving a theoretical answer, he told the story of the Good Samaritan, making it clear that "neighbor" means all those I come close to, no matter what their social or religious condition. Thus, whether others are enemies or neighbors is up to me. I can take an approach to life in which for me there are no enemies, and through care, forgiveness, and acceptance, all can be approached and become my neighbors.

The point where the break takes place is not between the self and the other, a suspected enemy, but between my consciousness and the drives roaring about within it. They are in me, but I am not fated to be their hostage. I can place them under the rule of care, reason, love, cooperation, and compassion. I can (and here lies the great spiritual challenge) accept death as an inherent part of life, as a wise invention of life itself that makes a qualitative leap beyond the coordinates of space and time toward a higher order of life, communication, and love.

Death lovingly accepted, as spiritual men and women of all ages attest, loses its sinister mask of archenemy of life. It is wondrously transformed into sister and opening to a higher life. Fear disappears. Freed from fear, consciousness feels at peace. Consciousness made peaceful is consciousness in freedom and perfect joy. Saint Francis of Assisi was one who achieved this ideal by welcoming death as sister. All human beings are capable of this if they are open to care, faith, hope, and love.

Why do most human beings not succeed in maintaining this understanding on a personal, social, and international level? Why do they continually need to create an enemy? Why do the lack of care, the fear of death, and the persistence of aggression continue so strongly to undermine the ways of peace? That remains an open question.

Lack of Peace: The Loss of Re-connection [re-ligação] with the Originating Fount

The third theory starts out from the many "whys" noted above. It seeks its source of illumination in another realm of human experience: encounter with the Mystery of God or with the God of Mystery. It is a theory that stems from the religious experience of humankind.

Native peoples from time immemorial and religious persons in all cultures have affirmed and continue to affirm the presence of a Mystery that permeates and enfolds existence and pervades the entire universe. They see it acting in the course of the stars, the tiniest movements of nature, the complexity of life, the sweep of human history, and especially in the depth of the human heart.

Its Word appears in a thousand languages. Human beings can interpret it, and amidst the many words, they can hear the Great Word of revelation. They feel that God dwells within them. They are filled with reverence and respect for every sign announcing God's presence.

Persons who have faith attest to the existence of a strand running through all beings and joining them like pearls so as to form a magnificent necklace. This strand is the ineffable Mystery, full of life and compassion. Such persons do not feel simply cast into existence: they know who they are, they feel they are placed into a great cosmic and earthly community and feel borne up by a Center of light and meaning that guides their life. Dying is not loss; it means a triumph of life itself. For men and women of faith in every generation what is affirmed by the Prayer of Saint Francis—"It is in dying that we are born to eternal life"—is existential truth.

Such persons dare to call this Mystery by a thousand names, aware that by any name it remains ever Mystery. They call it the One who walks with us (Yahweh), Isis, the Most High (Allah), the One who illumines (Deus), the One who is the way and goal (Tao), Shiva, Father and Mother of boundless kindness. The names are not important; what is important is the experience of the unifying Mystery.

Cultural expression of experience of the Mystery has given rise to the many religions. They are the institutional spaces where this experience is cultivated through rituals, celebrations, and doctrinal and ethical systems, projecting energizing ideals of justice, kinship, and happiness.

Experiencing this feeling of belonging to a greater whole means feeling umbilically connected and re-connected [re-ligado] to the divine heart that fills life with peace and serenity.

When is peace lost? When human beings lose the essential care and the blessed memory of this spiritual reconnection; when they identify God with something in this world; when injustice weakens intimacy with the Mystery; when religion, spiritual paths, and rituals are used with no realization that by themselves they are worthless. The result is loss of one's personal center, loss of peace.

Religions and spiritual traditions speak of the split running through human life from top to bottom. Christianity speaks of original sin as a state of sin, as a breaking away from the originating Fount. It is called "original," not in the sense of origins in time, but in the sense of the existential origin of the human being. Hence it is a sin that reaches to the origin and root of existence, the point where one connects to the whole and to God.

Building peace means taking the road back to the Fount, which goes by way of spirituality. It is spirituality that enables us to find God deep within all things, and provides the alphabet for de-coding the message that guides the human path.

By seeking the peace of God we can find human peace, a peace based on justice, love, and forgiveness, a peace that dispels from our horizon the fears that disturb us and rob us of inner peace.

The Prayer of Saint Francis seeks to make us instruments of peace, of that peace that emerges from the heart of God and that makes its way into the heart of all things.

This route is the most persuasive, the best attested by humankind, and the most universal. It is the route of the Prayer of Saint Francis. Let us follow it.

✚

Lord, remove all the obstacles hindering us along the way of your peace—envy, fear of death, and forgetfulness of your presence—by re-connecting all beings. Strengthen in us the energies of love, collaboration, and acceptance so that lasting peace may flourish among us. Amen.

What is peace?

We have discussed some of the reasons why we do not have peace. They have no doubt made us more willing to recite the Prayer of Saint Francis for Peace. But we do not want to simply stay at the point of removing hindrances to peace. We want to reach the realm of peace. What, then, is peace?

Peace cannot be defined simply in terms of ideas, because it has to do with values, which must be grasped more with the heart than with the head, through sensitivity more than through rationality.

In many countries and in great universities there are centers and institutes devoted to studying peace. As we read their reports and their many papers, we are puzzled at the way they ignore the spiritual dimensions of the pursuit of peace. Such writings accordingly do well enough in diagnosing problems, but they do not do well in setting forth actual proposals for peace. A minimal consensus about what is understood by peace is missing.

Here we are going to reflect on peace so as to be able to say the Prayer of Saint Francis with greater understanding.

Peace: Tranquillity of Order. What Order?

One definition of peace goes back to Saint Augustine (354–430) and has been part of all Christian thinking down to our own time. Papal documents on peace always mention it.

"Peace is the tranquillity of order," teaches the great North African doctor. Peace is the calm that comes from keeping and protecting the order intended by the Creator. When this order is violated, the result is discord and lack of peace, and society is torn apart.

In the opening sentence of his famous encyclical *Pacem in Terris* (1963), Pope John XXIII takes up the topic of peace as the tranquillity of order: "Peace on earth, which all men of every era have most eagerly yearned for, can be firmly established only if the order laid down by God is dutifully observed."

These lines are utterly clear, but are they not too abstract? Specifically, what is the order sought by God? This is the starting point for endless discussions among Christians and other major thinkers.

The Order Intended by the Creator: Medieval Christian Order?

For centuries the order intended by God was identified with the order proposed by the church: the regime of

Christendom, sustained by the wedding of throne and altar. The Kingdom of God was identified with the church, the church with the Christian world, and the Christian world with the world itself. Anyone who was against this order or outside it was regarded as an enemy of God and a tool of Satan. Heretics, Muslims, pagans, indigenous people were considered enemies of the order intended by God and were persecuted by the church. In the nineteenth century, liberator priests like Friar Caneca in Brazil and Morelos and Hidalgo who favored a republic in Mexico met the same fate and were excommunicated.

Around the world, whether by free acceptance or by force, everyone had to be brought into this assumed order. Under its aegis, as though under a single design—"spreading the faith of the empire"—the entire Amerindian and black hemisphere was colonized and made Christian. The violence brought to bear produced an enormous ethnocide; over the centuries, only one out of twenty-five Indians was left. One of the most respected missionaries in the Andes, Father José de Acosta, S.J. (sixteenth century) stated that "the new way of announcing the gospel is that of the missionary who arrives surrounded with soldiers and with full panoply." A Spanish colonist put it very well, "The voice of the gospel is heard only when the natives also hear the roar of firearms." Fear resulted in mass conversion.

Evangelization brought about by fear makes peace impossible. A sixteenth-century Mayan sage prophetically denounced the perversion:

"Oh, how we were saddened because they arrived
... sadness came into our midst ... Christianity was
introduced among us ... They taught us fear. They
came to kill the flowers. They killed our flower so
that only their flower would live."

This European Christian order presented as divine
order was false; it could not have come from God. God
was used to forge an ideology justifying world conquest.
All Christians became its accomplices. There were few ex-
ceptions, but they had a difficult time being heard. When
they were heard, they came under threat from the Inquisi-
tion. Not surprisingly, this order produced more death
than life, more war than peace.

The sixteenth-century Mayan prophet Chilam Balam
of Chumayel unmasked its claim to being the order intended by God: "Christians came here in large numbers
with the true God. But this meant the beginning of our
misery ... the beginning of our suffering ... This true God
who came from heaven speaks only of sin and his teaching
is only about sin."

Did not the Son of God through his incarnation come to
bring peace to all people of good will? Is not the gospel good
news, and hence a power producing harmony and peace?

The New World Economic Order: Natural Order?

A new world order is now in place. It also claims to be
natural, bound to the will of the Creator. This is an eco-

nomic order, namely the neoliberal world order with its capitalist mode of production and its globalized market. In the minds of its ideologists, there can be no alternatives to it. Everyone has to be brought in because outside it there is no salvation.

Hence, we are living under a single type of thought, the monotheism of the order of capital in its worldwide phase. Those who oppose it are immediately discounted as backwards, enemies of progress, obstructionists standing in the way of reaching the most advanced stage of history.

Yet the victims of this order unmask its perverse nature. They reject the idea that it is natural and inevitable. How can it be natural if it works for only 1.6 billion people, while the remaining 4 billion are excluded, enduring hunger and needlessly suffering from diseases that are curable? Is it natural that, to feed its insatiable production needs, this order is systematically attacking nature and causing the extinction of ten animal and fifty vegetable species each day?

Such an order can be maintained only with the massive use of force, violence in all its forms applied against those who resist and refuse to submit.

The question therefore remains: What is the order whose tranquillity produces peace?

We Are Responsible for Social Order-Action

Today more than in other times we are clearly conscious that we are historical beings and therefore live within an evolutionary process whose characteristic feature is not permanence but change. Orders are made by human beings. As we build meaning out of our lives, we relate among ourselves and with nature and with the traditions of the past, and we create orders that are open, dynamic, and changing so as to be able to live with a minimum of conviviality, justice, and peace.

All are called to collaborate in the creation of an order that includes as many people as possible and that promotes the continual pursuit of a balance of interests so that they will not be destructive of social peace. Such peace is the tranquillity of an *order-action* and not simply of an order closed in on itself whose stability is illusory.

"*Order-action*," as the expression itself suggests, means action that permanently creates human order, ever in process and hence ever capable of improvement. Such *order-action*, if fashioned in collective good will under the inspiration of an ethic of care open to the spiritual dimension of human beings, can approach the order intended by God.

Caring continually for such a dynamic order open to improvement can produce a minimum of the peace and tranquillity so yearned for by the sons and daughters of Earth.

Peace: Equilibrium of Movement. What Equilibrium?

The foregoing reflections make it easier for us to understand the second definition of peace: peace as equilibrium of movement. This notion comes from Pope Paul VI, who was a careful observer of changing world processes.

The notion of order as equilibrium of movement can be better understood if we situate it within the world view offered by the earth sciences, especially biology. Everything in the universe is in movement, because everything is organized in an all-encompassing play of relationships. The universe is more than the sum of all existing things. It is a dynamic combination, interwoven with chaos and cosmos, of relationships established in all directions and running through and sustaining everything.

Human societies and people's life histories are characterized by movement. We are subject to many processes that change us. We can grow with them, or we can sink because of them. Everything depends on how we assimilate them and how we find the balance suited to our drives and what we can incorporate constructively.

Recognizing what constitutes the balance of movement is a matter of existential wisdom. Principles and suggestions, the lessons of the great masters, the teachings of religions, and the knowledge provided by the sciences are absolutely necessary, but they are no substitute for the personal and group effort to find the balance suited to the people and community.

Gandhi, Rigoberta Menchú, Martin Luther King, and Dom Helder Camara, along with many other men and women, have well understood this in their views of active nonviolence: peace must be not only a goal but a method as well. Only peaceful means produce peace. Only people who are peaceful within themselves can actually bring about peace. The more serious the searching and the more dynamic the balance, the greater the chances for peace.

Peace: Consequence of Justice

A third understanding that has resonated greatly in history also comes from Saint Augustine: peace is the work of justice.

This definition recognizes that peace cannot be sought by itself without first achieving justice. There are many contemporary theories about justice. We will not go into discussing them. We will stick to one that is the most traditional, that has been accepted by major Christian thinkers and that goes back as far as Plato.

Justice is giving to each one his or her due. Justice is having a proper relation to each thing. Justice is therefore a correct relationship and stance, as required by each situation. In this sense we must have a minimum of knowledge about the things to which we relate and the situations with which we are faced in order to have proper and just relationships.

Justice means treating human beings as befits human beings: with acceptance, sympathy, and respect for their otherness. Justice means treating children as befits children: seeing that they have a home, watching over their innocence, providing health care and education. Justice means engaging in politics as it should be, namely, with care for the public realm. Justice means treating an animal as befits it: respecting its life, showing care for the conditions that allow it to live and reproduce, guaranteeing its place in the community of living things as a companion to human beings in the adventure of life. Justice means treating the sacred chalice as befits sacred things, storing it in a special and separate place with reverence for its symbolic character. Justice means treating garbage in a way befitting it, not putting it in the middle of the living room, but in a proper place, taking care to keep things properly clean. We could continue to exemplify other embodiments of justice.

Today social justice represents one of the most serious challenges to the conscience of the world. The abyss between those who are within the world "order" and those who are excluded is widening day by day. The use of leading-edge technologies has made it possible to accumulate wealth in a way that is fantastic but perverse because it is unjustly distributed. Twenty percent of humankind controls eighty percent of all means of life. That fact creates a dangerous imbalance in the movement of history.

If peace is equilibrium of movement, we are living in times of grave disequilibrium, of real war declared against the Earth, against ecosystems which are plundered, against peoples who are shunted aside because world capital is no longer interested in exploiting them, against whole classes of workers who are made expendable and excluded; war against the two-thirds of humankind who do not have the basic goods they need to live in peace. The world political movement does not show any equilibrium. Quite the contrary, imbalance in all areas is showing itself to be a threat to the common future of humankind and the earth.

When a society is organized around that which is fitting in each realm, then peace, the fruit of justice, can flourish.

Peace: Concord and Cordiality

Human beings do not live on justice alone, but also on freedom and generosity and the joy of being together as humans, friends, brothers, and sisters. It is out of this realm that *concord* arises.

The word *concord* is rich in meaning. It expresses the symphony of hearts (*cor*) beating at the same rhythm (*con*). When one heart listens to another, when it grasps not only what is evident but especially what is hidden, when hearts converge, there arises a mutual harmony or symphony, and the result is *concord*. *Concord* is another name for peace, the result of hearts in unison, in a single feeling, a single soul, a single spirit, a single aim, a single dream. Such *concord* does not cancel out differences, but it makes them converge beyond historic or cultural divergences.

Along with *concord* comes *cordiality*. *Cordiality* has to do with the heart (*cor*) and with its reason, as extolled by

Pascal. The reason of the heart places the person above self-interest, spiritual well-being above material well-being, peace above the need to be right. Human relations are always relations of feeling where the heart and its contradictions come into play. Out of the heart can arise prejudice and exclusion as well as the welcoming embrace and unifying love.

Peace is *cordiality* when persons and societies succeed in transforming existing relations of discrimination and domination into relationships of inclusion and equitable participation. The master-slave relationship, present in almost all social relations, is turned into a network of relationships between free citizens who care for one another mutually and deal with each other with *cordiality* and in an egalitarian manner. No doubt, peace as *concord* has a good deal of the utopian about it. But if we do not strive for the utopian, for the unattainable, we will not bring about what is "topian," what can be attained; if we do not yearn for the impossible, we will not reach the possible: everyday peace that fosters a modest but intense joy in living.

Your Peace—Our Peace:
Peace of God and Human Truce

Our reflections have shown not just a lack of peace in human history and in people's hearts, but also the fact that throughout history we have been unable to create for ourselves adequate conditions for allowing peace to emerge and to be assured. What is the future of the search for peace?

Here we discover the value of the Prayer of Saint Francis, because it is situated in the heart of another kind of peace that will make human peace possible. This is the peace of God, "your peace." Jesus tells us that the world cannot give it: "I leave you peace, I give you my peace; not as the world gives do I give it to you" (Jn 14:27). In what does God's peace consist?

Going directly to the core of the answer, we can say: it lies in the spirit of the beatitudes, embodied in the text of the Sermon on the Mount (Mt 5:1-12; Lk 6:20-26). This was the text that shaped Leo Tolstoy's stance of nonviolence. Gandhi drank from this text as he began his politics of active nonviolence. Martin Luther King Jr. imbibed from it to confront racial discrimination against blacks. It was this text that inspired Saint Francis in his pacifist movement throughout feudal Italy.

What is the essence of the spirit of the beatitudes? It is to refuse to grant the last word to evil, injury, persecution, and hatred, but to give it to love, forgiveness, mercy, kindness, and cordiality. The spirit of the beatitudes entails completely doing away with the category of "enemy," including every single person in care for one another, in mutual trust, and in love without borders.

As we confront the ambiguities of a reality in which the *diabolic* always goes along with the *symbolic*, the spirit of the beatitudes enables us to believe in the victory of the *symbolic*. The diseased portion of the human being (*dia-bolic*) can be healed by the sound part (*sym-bolic*).

The future is on the side of care, love, and forgiveness, never on the side of hatred and exclusion. It is pardon, love, and care that ground such peace as is possible, albeit ever threatened by the ongoing presence of hatred and ex-clusion. Hence, the positive side must be strengthened. It has enough energy to limit the power of aggression to cause division.

Pardon means removing one who has offended us from the category of offender. As a person, he or she is more than one who wrongs, and has potentialities that can and must be rescued. Hence, to forgive is to draw him or her out of the solitude that produces injury, and to transform him or her into a being of communication and loving friendship.

Such an attitude is one of pure gratuity, and is com-pletely unconditional. Love cannot expect reward. It loves for the sake of loving, as a flower that blooms in order to bloom.

Because it has this structure of gratuity, love is always characterized by a "not so much...as to," typified in the experience of Jesus, and so well expressed in the Prayer of Saint Francis: "Grant that I may not so much seek to be consoled as to console; to be understood, as to understand; to be loved, as to love." Through this "not so much...as to" the human being emerges stronger than he or she would from any conditioning, and is able to keep loving even when there is no return.

This "not so much...as to" reveals the self-surpassing capability of human beings, a way of being that leaves the world of resentment and self-centeredness behind so as to move out toward others without asking who they are, what they are like, where they come from, or what their moral condition is. This is the way of being of the Creator, who lets the sun and the rain fall on good and evil, just and unjust, who loves the ungrateful and evil (Lk 6:35). This is a foundational attitude of divine peace that should inspire human peace. It has no preconditions. It is a peace with no enemies.

Human peace left to the mercy of the ambiguity of our situation is more a truce between belligerent parties than a true peace between them. It is a pause during which each goes back over past battles and prepares to renew the struggle. A truce takes place in the context of war. No war is holy, just, and clean. All wars are inhumane and perverse.

True peace cannot be based on one-sided reasons, for they fuel the conflict. Peace emerges only when there is care and cooperation between cultures, nations, political leaders, artists, thinkers, religious people, and all human beings, men and women.

All our observations speak the truth about peace. But the truth of peace must be *done*. Then peace will move from head to heart, from heart to hands, and from hands to social, economic, political, and ecological processes so that they will achieve a proper balance in their movement and produce a sustainable peace.

Lord, make us builders of an order that is guided by the justice and cordiality that can bring peace to the world. Give us a sense of dynamic equilibrium so your peace may be in our intentions, in the means we use, and in the ends for which we yearn. Amen.

How to be an instrument of your peace?

What does being an instrument mean? We have to understand "instrument" in an existential rather than a mechanical way. A mechanical understanding regards an instrument as something separate from what it serves. For example, using a ladder as an instrument, I reach a cluster of bananas up there. But the nature of a ladder has nothing to do with the bananas. It is merely a material instrument used to pick the cluster of bananas.

Being an instrument of peace is not the same. Those who want to be instruments of God's peace must be themselves peaceful persons, steeped in essential care and filled with the spirit of the beatitudes, which is what brings peace. From within themselves they must radiate a peace rooted in their deepest identity.

Consider a samba dancer, a mulatta from the hills of Rio de Janeiro, with her perfect body and her bearing like that of an African princess, dancing to carnival music. Her body, her legs, and her waist are not mere instruments at the service of the samba beat, they embody the rhythm and the dancing. Her steps, the graceful play of her legs, and the swaying of her waist are not instruments of the rhythm and the music—they are the rhythm and the music; they embody the sound and become a form of full human communication. Her body itself becomes spirit, such is her virtuosity and her identification with the music.

We find the same thing in a passionate violinist. His whole body bends over the instrument. His arms enwrap it, as though caressing it, and his fingers skim over the strings with agility, fingering with such spontaneity and grace that it all seems to be one thing: the musician, his body, the violin, strings, fingers, rhythm, and music. Everything is a living instrument of music.

We become instruments of God's peace when we are so permeated that we do not even think about it. We radiate peace and good will, we communicate kindness and a loving attitude because God's peace becomes flesh of our flesh.

Saint Francis, Instrument of God's Peace

We find an example of peace in person in Saint Francis of Assisi. Biographies dating from his own time, such as those of Thomas of Celano, Saint Bonaventure, the *Legend of the Three Companions*, and the Perusine Legend, all say that he was a man in whom the structure of desire reached supreme expression. Saint Bonaventure calls him simply *vir desideriorum*, man of desires.

As we know, desires are inherently unlimited and in conflict. How to integrate to them? How to calm them? What example does Saint Francis pass on to us?

Peace with Himself

The *Legend of the Three Companions*, one of the most authentic witnesses to Saint Francis, shows his strategy: make a fundamental desire central and integrate every-thing else around it. To find his core desire, he "went to take counsel with the wise and the simple, the perfect and the imperfect, the great and the little, seeking to find out from them how he could most easily reach the peak of per-fection." He discovered that the way to it is the gospel of the lowly, lived out literally, without comments that would water it down. He called this road the way of sim-plicity. Happy the one who has discovered it, he exclaims: "This is what I ardently desire; it is this that I aspire to with all the sincerity of my heart . . . this is what I desire to put into practice with all my strength."

In Saint Francis we note the highest form of mimetic desire. He wanted to follow and imitate Jesus in the small-est details, and he acted on this to the point of wanting to be one with Christ. In receiving the stigmata at the end of his life, he achieved his fundamental mimetic desire. Here mimetic desire is not confrontation with a rival to seize the object of desire away from him. It is an encounter with the archetype of the Master whom he wants to follow and love so radically that it allows for an experience of non-duality, of identification. Is not this what mystics like Saint Bonaventure, Saint John of the Cross, and Saint Teresa attest to?

To reach this point of identification, Francis realizes that he must calm the volcanic force of desire that seizes him from within. One of the things that he most implores God for in his prayers is to be able to integrate his desires. He begs for the grace of winning peace of heart, for his heart is always torn by ambiguity, by the struggle between the *symbolic* and the *diabolic*. The penances to which he subjects himself are not pain-seeking self-flagellation, but a way of conquering himself and winning inner freedom.

This freedom required many sacrifices because the *daimon* dwelling in him—that inner energy of enthusiasm and strength that permeated him—almost broke the limits of his own body. At the end of his life he recognized that, with God's grace and with self-control, he was reaching *concord* between spirit and body, between the will to ascend and the desires of the body. When a fellow friar admiringly commented on how diligently his body obeyed him, he replied: "I can attest that my body was always obedient... it only wanted to comply with what I ordered. On this point, it and I are completely in agreement [*con-cordes*]: we serve the Lord Jesus Christ with no disdain."

Peace in the Community of Brethren

From being a man of desire, Saint Francis became a man of peace. With God's peace instilled in him, he was able to undertake the mission of peace, as he himself understood his own peacemaking activity and that of the group that he created around himself. It was a true pacifist movement in the modern sense. In his testament he said clearly, "The Lord revealed to me that we should greet one another by saying, 'The Lord give you peace.'" Wherever they went, he and his companions used this greeting, or another one that has prevailed to this day, "Peace and goodness."

First of all, Saint Francis wanted peace to be lived out in the relationships of his own companions. He always called them "my brothers," "my most beloved brothers," or "my blessed brothers," expressions of extreme affection that do not allow any room for divisions or exclusion.

Despite this affection, the *diabolic* dimension also made its way into the communities of brothers. Conflicts can always occur; the problem lies not in conflicts but in how they are handled. To the superior of a religious house who was upset with such situations, and who wrote to him complaining, Saint Francis sent the following response, a true peace strategy:

"Love those who act against you with violence, and do not ask of them anything but what the Lord gives you. And it is precisely in this that you

must love them, not even desiring that they become better Christians. And this is more valuable
to you than life in a hermitage. And in this will I
recognize that you really love the Lord and me, his
servant and yours, if you do the following: let there
be no brother in the world, even should he have
sinned to the maximum, who after looking you in
the eyes feels perhaps obliged to leave your presence without obtaining mercy, if he sought mercy.
And if he did not seek mercy, ask him whether he
wants to receive it. And if after that he comes before your eyes a thousand times, love him more
than me, seeking to win him for the Lord. And always have mercy on such brothers."

This reply, which is found in the *Letter to a Minister of
the Friars Minor*, represents an instance of the highest spirituality that the Western tradition has produced, a page of
pure evangelization. It is the gospel of peace through unconditional love and unlimited forgiveness, with no preconditions. It can lead only to the inauguration of the
messianic kingdom of God's peace.

Peace in Unequal Society

The peace that Francis wanted to attain was not re-
stricted solely to relations between persons. We know that
the forms of structural violence that leave the largest

numbers of victims take place within social relationships. The society of his time was deeply divided into greater and lesser, clergy and lay, nobility and commoners. Conflicts between them were continual and towns frequently went to war against each other.

Saint Francis disarms conflicts with goodness and gentleness. He harbors no resentment toward others whose options are different from his own, such as the rich. The *Legend of the Three Companions* says that he was insistent with his fellow friars that "no one judge anyone or look with contempt on those who live in luxury and whose dress is fancy and ostentatious, because God is Lord over them and us and has the power to call them to Himself and make them just."

About prelates living dissolute lives, he said, "I want to convert them through holy humility and reverence for them."

He won over the robbers who were ambushing people in order to get food by going after them and shouting to them, "Brother robbers, come to us. We are friars and we bring you excellent wine and delicious bread." And he would spread out the small tablecloth on the ground and eat with them. Afterwards, he would urge them, "When you lay ambush, for the love of God, do not abuse people." Touched by such kindness, they put aside their outlaw life, and some joined religious houses.

The conversion of the wolf of Gubbio is a metaphor for Saint Francis's stance toward an exploiter and toward a

whole band of oppressors who were intimidating and steal-
ing from the people of the city. His strategy is not a harsh
attack on oppression, but a sweet and soft approach
through dialogue, an appeal to the sensitivity that always
exists in people, and the certainty that collaboration is
more effective than competition. An agreement is reached
between the wolf of Gubbio and the citizens: all must ad-
just mutually so that none will be in need and all may live
in peace.

Saint Francis was able to make peace even in highly
contentious situations, such as those in Bologna, Arezzo,
Sienna, and especially in his native city, Assisi. This last
was particularly moving. On his deathbed he heard that
there was a conflict between the mayor of the city and the
bishop, who had excommunicated the mayor, who in turn
had prohibited anyone in the city from having anything to
do with the bishop. The feud was tearing the city apart.
Invoking the moral authority that he enjoyed and even
though he was terminally ill, Francis got to work asking
both of them, bishop and mayor, to meet in front of the
bishop's palace. There he sent two of his fellow friars, asking them to sing the Canticle to Brother Sun on his behalf, adding a specially prepared verse: "Praised be you,
My Lord, for those who forgive for your love and bear with
illnesses and tribulations. Blessed be those who maintain
peace and who will be crowned by You the Most High."

The effect was immediate. They forgave and hugged
one another effusively. The people went wild seeing the

miracle wrought by their greatest son, the *poverello* and *fratello*, instrument of social peace.

Enduring Peace with Nature and with Mother Earth

Peace would be incomplete unless it also encompassed the world. Francis showed such devotion and reverence for nature that he established an enduring peace with the Earth, which he loved as mother and sister, and with all creatures of the Earth. Thomas of Celano, his first biographer, marvelously sums up this ecological stance of Saint Francis:

> He was filled with ineffable joy whenever he saw the sun, contemplated the moon, and directed his gaze at the stars and the firmament... When he was with flowers, he preached to them, as though they were endowed with intelligence, and he called on them to praise the Lord. He did it with most tender and moving simplicity: he urged gratitude on the wheat fields and vineyards, the stones and the forests, the plains and river currents, the beauty of the gardens, the earth, fire, air and wind. Finally, he sweetly called all creatures sisters, and in a marvelous way that no one understood he divined their secrets, like one who already enjoys the freedom and glory of the sons of God.

This attitude of reverence and affection led him to pick snails up from the roads so they would not be trodden under foot. In winter he gave honey to bees so they would not die of want and cold. He asked his brethren not to cut trees down to the root with the hope that they could regenerate and grow again. Indeed, he felt that spaces ought to be reserved in gardens for weeds so that they could survive, because "they also proclaim the most splendid Father of all beings."

One could not live so intimately with all beings unless one had heard their symbolic resonance in one's soul, connecting environmental ecology with an ecology of the heart, and had never situated oneself above things but at their feet, truly as brother and sister, discovering the bonds of kinship linking all things. We are all umbilically tied to our motherly Father, creator and universal provider. Awareness of this leads to an imperturbable peace, with no fear from threats, the peace of one who feels at home with one's parents, brothers, and sisters.

The Supreme Form of Peace: Complete Self-denial

The supreme expression of peace, comprised of patience, understanding, and forgiveness, is symbolized by the well-known story of perfect joy. Through this imaginative device, Saint Francis portrays all kinds of injuries and violence against two companions (one of them Saint

Francis himself) who, soaked in rain and mud, come to the priory. There the porter rejects them and beats them with a stick. Although recognized as fellow friars, they are morally vilified and rejected as evildoers.

In the story of perfect joy, Francis step by step dismantles the mechanisms that generate the culture of violence and lays the foundations for the culture of peace. True joy is not found in self-esteem nor in the need for recognition, nor in performing miracles and speaking in tongues. Rather, it is found in love and forgiveness, in reconciliation beyond any precondition or demand. Only then does perfect joy break through. This joy is the source of an unchangeable inner peace, able to live happily with the harshest contradictions, peace as the fruit of utter abnegation. Is this peace not the first fruit of the Reign of justice and love?

Francis was a personal instrument of peace, of the peace that God desires for humankind. For Francis, peace did not remain mere empty desire, or mere intention [proposta]. It was a radical response [res-posta] by the work and grace of the Mystery and by the humble and good-natured collaboration of one of the most outstanding human beings produced by Christianity, Francis of Assisi.

After all these considerations, we can understand the dimension of the challenge placed before us: that we also be instruments of peace in a world troubled by all kinds of disruptions and conflicts.

Lord, make us instruments of your peace as we seek to live in peace with ourselves, with the community closest to us, with others in our unequal society, and in the midst of the worst conflicts. May we be able to strive to bear tensions and contradictions, seeking to maintain communion with all creatures and making your peace visible. Amen.

Where there is hatred,
let me sow love

The personal and social life of human beings is moved by two great passions: love and hatred. Saint Augustine projected his conception of universal history onto these two powerful forces: love which leads to the death of self for the sake of the other and hatred which leads to the death of the other for the sake of self. Love founds the City of God, where human beings feel brought, as it were, into a great womb. Hatred founds the city of Satan, where human beings devour one another as in a prison.

In our world, these two cities—these two types of society —blend together and are found in one another. Love and hatred are like the wheat and tares that grow together inseparably in a field. This helps us understand why love is never solely love: it is continually accompanied by the shadow of possible antipathy and indifference toward others. Conversely, hatred is never just hatred: it is always accompanied by some compassion, some affectionate feeling, and some signs of bad conscience and repentance.

Thank God, we never manage to be completely evil. Otherwise we would sink into absolute perdition. In fact, we are like parachutes, always falling softly and slowly. And in this soft fall we can retrieve the dimension of love that lies hidden in the enterprise of hatred.

What makes human, personal, and social life dramatic is the coexistence of love and hatred. Sometimes hatred prevails over love. Persons, groups, and peoples allow the feelings of rejection, exclusion, and death to flourish. Things begin in the heart: that is where prejudice is nourished, evil intentions nestle, and aversion develops. Then comes continuity in attitudes: acts of rejection, exclusion, and death are considered. Matters finally reach the hands. They lend themselves to violence, torture, ethnic cleansing, murder, and wars of extermination. Hatred is an overwhelming destructive energy.

Sometimes love prevails over hatred. The heart is tender and loving; attitudes are well-intentioned and welcoming; actions are constructive and in solidarity. People embrace, groups cooperate, and peoples respect and esteem one another. Love moves the heavens and all the stars (Dante). Love is God's proper name (Saint John).

How to face up to the power of hatred? Suppressing it does not work; contemplation is not enough; self-control is insufficient. Only love overcomes hatred. Love alone dismantles strategies of rejection, because love is the energy of unlimited inclusion. Even when it does not encounter love, love forgives and enwraps the enemy internally. No force can overpower the tenderness of a look and the affection of a hug. Saint Paul attests to it in his famous hymn to love: Love "bears all things, believes all things, hopes all things, endures all things. Love never ends" (1 Cor 13:7-8).

What are we to do so that love may overcome hatred? We must take a basic approach to life in which love is the central axis, in which the power inspiring our desires and our actions, from the simplest to the highest, comes from love. Love must permeate our whole life. Whatever is produced bears the traces of love, just as the newborn baby reveals traces of the mother and father.

Love does not win all the battles. It experiences defeats —but it wins the decisive final battle. The end-point of all the struggles of human existence is the loving embrace between all when they acknowledge one another as neighbors, as brothers and sisters. Suffering passes away, hatred passes away. In the end, only love remains, warming hearts, guiding history ahead and upward, for it is the life and joy of eternity.

✠

Lord, where there is hatred let me sow love. Make us draw out of ourselves the love hidden under the ashes of secret hatreds. May our love for others stir up the love hidden within them that can transform hatred. Make love set our hearts on fire, shine forth in our attitudes, and be embodied in our actions, so that hatred will have no more place in us. Amen.

Where there is injury,
let me sow pardon

The dominant history is dominant because it is fashioned by the winners. They have poets who sing their victories, artists who raise monuments to them, and historians who enshrine their memory. But who listens to the voices of the victims unjustly wronged and defeated?

The injuries come in countless forms and appear in endless guises. For ten thousand years women have been suffering under patriarchal male culture. They have been, and are, especially wronged because they are not recognized for their inestimable labor in reproducing life, educating their children, and passing on with their mother's milk the values that sustain the culture. They make history, but even when they occupy a significant portion of the labor market, and lead or take part in social movements, they are usually kept off the stage and invisible. Men forget that they were born from women.

Native peoples on the various continents have been wiped out in hopeless wars or have disappeared through forced integration and assimilation. Wrongs are piled upon wrongs.

Millions and millions of Africans were perversely torn from their lands and taken as slaves to be consumed like coal in the production process of whites—a wrong that is historically irreparable.

The poor of the world are continually wronged in their dignity, for they are denied the right to a basic citizenship that would assure them the minimum for survival. Countless community, labor, political, and religious leaders have been and are still being unjustly imprisoned, tortured, exiled, and assassinated because of their struggle for elementary justice.

Until the last judgment all these humiliated and injured have the right to claim justice and recognition for their cause.

There remains the everyday, anonymous injury that takes place in interpersonal and social relations, when someone tries to put others down, destroy their image, and intentionally humiliate them.

How to bring pardon where so much injury thrives? Above all, the oppressors are indebted to all the victims that they have created through history, a debt in justice. Women still do not occupy their rightful place in society, native peoples still do not till their own lands, and blacks who were once enslaved even today have not received any compensation whatsoever. They all remain humiliated and wronged.

There is still a need to ask forgiveness. Heads of states and representatives of the ruling classes must solemnly, truly, and formally ask for forgiveness for the wrongs inflicted on millions of people over the centuries. Such a gesture entails recognition of a guilt that is repaired only by policies of compensation and by efforts to retrieve the memory, values, and cultures that have been silenced.

But there is a forgiveness that the humiliated and injured are themselves invited to grant. Here lies the potential greatness and magnanimity of the human heart. Forgiving those who have offended does not mean forgetting the blows and wounds received. It is the ability to see wrongdoers not just as wrongdoers, but as human beings who are to be pitied for the evil that they have perpetrated, while at the same time realizing that they are bearers of a potential that can turn them into friends and kin. Forgiving means opening them to this possibility.

This is how we overcome the dichotomy between oppressed and oppressor and injurer and injured. We will then find ourselves on the same human ground from which we must together build a world where there is room for reconciliation and forgiveness, and where mutual care, kinship, solidarity, and mutual respect constitute the permanent foundations for shared life.

Lord, where there is injury, let me sow forgiveness. On that day when you are going to weigh our history, forgive those who have wronged and humiliated our brothers and sisters, for they too are your sons and daughters. But give us strength so that we will never do ourselves what they have done. Rather, make us people of solidarity, compassion, and unlimited love. Amen.

Where there is discord,
let me sow union

Discord tears the social fabric and the hearts of human beings on many levels. There is discord between nations over economic disputes, there are border definition issues, ideological conflicts, and age-old resentments. All these carry the seeds of war, which is the supreme expression of discord.

Discord afflicts social classes in conflict over contending interests. The winners want to gain more, and those who gain more never have enough. This voracious greed gives rise to tensions that break the minimum bonds of justice and involvement in the same history and in a shared destiny.

How often the shadowy forces win the game! They create division to serve domination. They pit some against others to weaken them and more easily rule over them all. Is not this the policy preferred by the powerful of the world? Is this not what old and new colonizers have done, splitting ethnic groups apart, creating different countries and setting them up to wage war among themselves, wear one another out, and leave their real enemy, the colonizer, untouchable?

Often enough, discord exists between members of the same family. Brothers hate brothers, sisters hate mother and children, and daughters want their parents to die in order to inherit the fortune they have amassed.

Discord reaches into the depths of the human heart when it allows itself to be taken over by hatred, evil intentions, and the will to revenge. It is a struggle waged between the *diabolic* and the *symbolic*. The *diabolic* seeks to divide and to do evil. The *symbolic*, aware of this evil, seeks to re-tie bonds and *re-connect* [*re-ligar*] what has been shattered. People feel they are in an arena where angels and devils do battle, each seeking to dominate the entire field.

Despite the drama of this situation, one of the deepest yearnings of the spirit is the striving for concord between desire and heart, between heart and reality, and between reality and the originating Source of all beings. Human beings need to be grounded in this union in order to guide themselves and not feel exiled in a world full of contradictory signs.

What does it mean to sow union where there is discord? First of all, it means eliminating the causes that lead to discord. The primary cause is personal and social injustice; it destroys relations of friendship between people and tears the fabric of society. One who is committed to the changes

necessary for changing unjust relations, and who participates in or supports movements that in an organized way
are seeking justice, is creating the conditions for union.

Understanding and tolerance are fundamental if there
is to be union between peoples, union in a world of differences. Understanding implies overcoming any rigidity of
opinion and any kind of dogmatism. It entails being open
to new views and making them compatible with one's
own. Hence the importance of tolerance. Tolerance does
not mean approving everything or accepting what cannot
be changed. It means the ability to respect the positions of
others and to live happily with them. Only one who re-
spects others earns the right to question and criticize them
and to even oppose them. Tolerance makes possible coexistence with differences, mutual enrichment, convergence
in diversity, and a union that is dynamic and open to new
contributions.

Sowing union where there is discord ultimately entails
applying a holistic vision of reality. Everything in the universe and in history has to do with everything else and is
unified in the heart of God. Nothing is by chance. A divine design interweaves all processes and composes a symphony with all the notes, even those that are most out of
tune, and in such a way that there is only one history, a
history of creation and salvation, a history of humaniza-
tion and divinization.

This comprehensive vision of the unity of history enables us to say, like the Eastern sages and the Christian

mystics: the heart of the universe, the heart of the flower, the heart of life, the heart of the human being, and the heart of God are—at their deepest core—one thing. They are ever united dynamically and in convergence.

Where there is discord, let me sow union. Give us thirst for justice, understanding, and tolerance so that we may live joyfully with one another. Give us a heart that feels the beating of the heart of the universe and of every creature, a beating that is in tune with your divine heart that unites all, diversifies all, and makes all converge. Amen.

Where there is doubt,
let me sow faith

There are many kinds of doubts. There are doubts in our understanding of the reality around us, due to its great complexity. The contemporary view of the world holds that reality is always in transformation and in inter-action with the most varied factors, building the dynamic equilibrium necessary so that everything may function harmoniously. In this process there are ambiguities, forks in the road, probabilities that may or may not come about. Here there are few certainties and many doubts. Where is humankind going? Will there be more good will toward Earth and therefore assurance of a hopeful future? Doubts and more doubts abound. We may be headed toward great dilemmas, with the possibility of widespread devastation of nature as countless living organisms and millions of people are destroyed.

There are even more wrenching doubts: can we expect that humankind will learn to accept itself as a great family that is concerned for all its members from widely varying

traditions, cultures, and religions, and that all will help
one another as loving brothers and sisters do? Why do the
physically and mentally handicapped and their families
have to suffer so much? Can we hope that social classes
will overcome their antagonisms and from their differences produce not tensions, conflicts, and wars, but rather
stimulation, collective searching for what is best, and a
new social energy?

Some doubts reach as far as the core of our hope and
the ultimate meaning of our life. What can we expect
after this life? Will there be someone there to receive us,
to wipe away our tears and bring us into a happy home?
Who will do justice for the millions of those annihilated
over so many centuries for the sake of greed, or power, or
vengeance? Will there be someone who will have compassion on our iniquities and forgive us completely? Who will
be able to banish all our uncertainties and take away all
our doubts? What spiritual master? What sage? What
saint?

It is out of the anguish of such doubts that faith gains
meaning. There are two types of faith that must be lived
out concretely: faith-trust and faith-belief.

First comes faith-trust, a stance of complete surrender
to Someone Greater, to the creator of the universe, who
burns in our heart as enthusiasm (in Greek *en-theos-mos* =
enthusiasm, which means a God within), giving us energy
to live, struggle, overcome obstacles, and hope. This radical trust gives us serenity and peace. It dispels all doubts.

Through it we realize that we are in the hands of a kind Father and Mother. From the height of the cross Jesus lived this faith-trust. His last words were not, "Father, why have you abandoned me?" but "Father, into your hands I commend my spirit."

Then comes faith-belief, acceptance of God's historic revelation and plan of communion. Through the prophets, and through spiritual masters and persons of all creeds and cultures, God has communicated himself to humankind and revealed himself as the One who desires companions in love. In the history of the Jews and of Christians, for example, he has revealed himself as a God who has established a covenant of communion with all humankind, giving us the certainty that we are really his sons and daughters. Even more, he came to feel so ardently about human beings that he wanted to be one of them. He became incarnate in our weak and limited flesh. And when he saw that we rejected him, he surrendered his life out of love to win us back. His effort has proven worthwhile, because he arose to show us that this love of his cannot be frustrated. It cannot end with death on the cross. We will all be raised up with him and like him.

This faith-belief settles all doubts about our future. Even on our deathbed, should our hearts accuse us, a stronger voice will make itself heard, assuring us: "God is greater than our hearts. He is love. He is forgiveness. And full of faith, we will die in peace, falling into the arms of a motherly Father and fatherly Mother."

Lord, where there is doubt, let me sow faith. Do not allow doubt to extinguish the guiding stars that shed light on our way. Give us faith-trust which places us in your hands. Grant us faith-belief in your design which seeks to have us united in your kingdom together with all creation. Amen.

Where there is error,
let me sow truth

One human trait that bears the heaviest consequences is human fallibility. Human beings can be wrong often and in many ways. There are countless kinds of errors.

Some errors are caused by *ignorance* of the universe, about the Earth, and about life. We know very little about our cosmic dwelling. We can be filled with enchantment over the starry sky, but most people are unaware of how it was formed out of a minuscule speck of highly concentrated matter and energy that exploded at a certain point. Within the large red stars that then took shape were elaborated the one hundred or so physical-chemical elements that make up all beings, including our own bodies. Once we were all there together: energy fields, elementary particles, hydrogen, helium, iron, nitrogen, everything that is now part of our material universe.

Some errors flow from *illusion* about ourselves. We are often mistaken in our self-image, considering ourselves to be less when actually we are more, with much positive potential. At other times we are wrong about the angels and devils dwelling in us, the passions and desires that make it necessary for us to have discipline and self-control, so as to integrate them and grow harmoniously.

Some errors about others take the form of *prejudice*. Rather than learning about others through personal contact and open dialogue, we easily pigeonhole them in preconceived categories, failing to recognize their value and to give them a friendly welcome. In the age of Saint Francis, Pope Urban II, who organized crusades, viewed the Saracens in a distorted way as "vile, degenerate, and servants of the devil." Saint Francis, after meeting with them and conversing with the sultan, said: "They are our brothers and friends, and we must love them very much." Only existential truth destroys error and prejudice.

Some errors are caused by *alienation* from our place and our mission on Earth and in the universe. Within the evolutionary process, we are that point at which the universe comes to itself and grasps the thread running through all. We are not just *on* the Earth; we *are* the Earth—feeling, thinking, loving, and revering. Our mission is to be able to grasp the meaning permeating everything, and to utter the word of praise that can be the echo of the Great Word vibrating in every being. Saint Francis did so in an exemplary manner in his Canticle to Brother Sun. Most people live in alienation, thinking that they only exist to work, work to accumulate, and accumulate in order to enjoy.

Some errors are *sin* against God. It is sin to consciously deny God's divine presence in the cosmos and in human history. It is sin not to voluntarily recognize God in the depths of each person. It is sin against God to violate, torture, and murder human beings, his image and likeness. Sin causes us to lose God. In losing God, we lose the magic, the enchantment, and the ultimate meaning of life and the universe.

Sowing truth means more than announcing true messages. It means creating conditions of transparency and justice so that the truth may emerge by itself and display its liberating and creative light.

We sow truth to the extent that we make ourselves true and transparent in words, deeds, attitudes, and intentions. Nothing is less suited to the nature of truth than the arrogance and pretension of always being right. Truth is like light: it has its own certain intensity. Too much light is blinding. Likewise, too much truth is worse than error, as Blaise Pascal said a long time ago. It is only in the proper measure that truth dispels darkness and error.

✠

Lord, where there is error, let me sow truth. Grant that we may be courageous in uncovering our errors, especially those that obscure your presence in all things. May the truth shine through our sincere hearts, our humanizing gestures, our pure intentions, and our ongoing pursuit of fidelity and truth. Never allow us to oppress others in the name of religious truth. Amen.

Where there is despair, let me sow hope

Actual human beings are comprised of various energy centers that give life its dynamic quality: desire, the survival instinct, care, love, capacity for grasping wholes. One of the main energy centers is that of hope, understood not simply as a virtue but as a principle giving rise to many virtues. Hope is the basic energy driving all the others.

We can lose faith, and if we do, the result is a terrifying absence of meaning. But life goes on. We can lose love, and then the luster and joy in living disappear. But people keep going and seek a new love. When we lose hope, however, all reasons for living vanish. Insanity, suicide, and death are the ghosts swirling about those who lose hope. This is the hell of despair.

Scenes of despair are horrifying: eyes protrude, faces are deformed, people throw themselves out of tall buildings, they jump into a stormy sea, they drive their cars off cliffs. Out of fear of dying, desperate people sometimes kill themselves. Despair arises when the person is placed in a situation with no exit and feels corralled and up against the wall.

Among the many situations of despair two stand out today: dire social poverty and the awareness that death is near and inevitable. Over a billion people live below the line of absolute poverty. The huge numbers should not blind us to the despair of individual people who do not know what they are going to eat, where they will sleep, and how they will manage to reach the next day. What is most painful is to see one's children suffering hunger and not know where to turn. Solidarity between human beings is scarce. When future generations look back at our age, they are going to condemn us as barbaric, inhumane, and merciless, because we were insensitive to the sufferings of our brothers and sisters.

How many go into despair when they discover that a person they love has AIDS or that a child's cancer has spread into the main vital organs? The horizon of the future closes. Death casts its mortal shadow over life.

The idea of a death foretold is one of the most difficult things for the human spirit to absorb. The first feeling is one of injustice: why me, why him or her, when there are so many evildoers who deserve to die first? Next comes revolt: why die now rather than completing the cycle of life? Then there is self-victimization: the person feels that he or she is an innocent victim of uncontrollable mechanisms of nature or of the body itself, which suddenly becomes alien and traitorous. Then all possible approaches

to a cure are attempted. Hope is stirred up that there may
be physicians, folk healers, people with extra-sensory pow-
ers or secret knowledge who can save us. When nothing
deters death's destructive work, the person surrenders and
becomes resigned. Even so, miracles occur—not always
the cure so desperately sought after, but the re-fashioning
of the meaning of life through a peaceful surrender to
God. Because of faith, death can cease to be a terrifying
specter and can become serene liberation.

How to sow hope? In the face of situations of injustice,
it is in concretely engaging against them that we find the
grounds for hope. Victorious processes of change—as modest as they might be—always open a new horizon of hope
which gives meaning to life and struggle.

At those times when people are left on their own, the
important thing, rather than many words, is to communicate an aura of calm and confidence to the despairing.
This aura is gained only by internalizing convictions so
powerful that they become part of our being: we are in
the embrace of the infinitely kind Father and Mother,
into whose care we can surrender. Whether the winds are
from behind or ahead, God will guide our boat safely to
harbor.

The path of life may be stormy, but the end is good
and is already guaranteed by the certainty of resurrection
and the promise of eternal life. The phoenix arises from
the ashes and from the shadows of death through hope in
a happy transfigured life beyond the present one.

Lord, where there is despair, may I sow hope. May I be in solidarity with the struggle of those who seek justice. May I know how to create an atmosphere of unlimited confidence in your mysterious design of love. Inspire me with words to arouse the ineffable hope of living forever in your home with all those who have gone before us in history. Amen.

Where there is sadness, let me sow joy

Saint Paul subtly distinguishes between two types of sadness: worldly sadness, which produces death, and godly sadness, which produces life (2 Cor 7:10).

One type of worldly sadness is that which results from forced joy aimed at deceiving people. Advertising holds up success at any cost, exalts the use and consumption of certain products, going to fashionable places, and being with celebrities. Someone who smokes a certain brand of cigarettes is induced to feel that he or she is in a marvelous setting, traveling in a glittering Ferrari. The cigarette claims to work automatically, independent of the person's will, bringing the promised benefits. But the fact is that any cigarette does damage, contaminates one's lungs, and befouls the atmosphere. The promise is a lie, for it causes frustration and worldly sadness, and does not produce the happiness it promises.

Another worldly sadness comes from envy. Envying others means wishing that they did not have the good that they have. By simply having it, they cause inconsolable sadness in the envious one who will do whatever it takes to make them lose that good. This worldly sadness produces existential death, negation of the meaning of life.

But there is godly sadness. It arises when we contemplate God's design and see it being frustrated in history. We experience godly sadness when we realize that a death machine is operating against the Earth and its physical and chemical balance, against the splendor of its forests and the complexity of its biodiversity. Countless species of living beings are threatened with extinction. Godly sadness arises from our awareness that the divine design is being frustrated and from our reverence for the good creation that is being destroyed.

We are filled with heartrending sadness when we see thousands upon thousands of street children, boys and girls, filthy, sleeping out in the open, yearning for a kind gesture, and in danger of being wiped out by death squads. Our sadness is just as great when we see ill people vainly looking for help, older people waiting in long lines to receive their tiny pensions after a whole life of work. This is godly sadness, because we are looking at the divine image and likeness obscured and a denial of the basic respect owed to the humanity of innocent children, the sick, and older people.

Our sadness is godly when we become aware of parts of ourselves that are not integrated and of the unraveling of our personal core due to a life of injustice, hypocrisy, and selfishness. This sadness comes from the realization that we have betrayed the appeals of our ethical conscience and have opposed God's will.

How are we to sow joy? It cannot be sown directly, because joy cannot be given. Joy results from many actions, carried out with a wholesome intention, with care, and with a desire to act rightly in order to bring about change.

I believe that no better example can be proposed than the work of a literacy team of the Landless Movement (MST) as they carry out their Paulo Freire-inspired consciousness-raising methodology. The group organizes young people and works with them over an eight-month period, teaching them and instructing them in the "generative words" (rights to land, housing, and health care). Group members give their all, despite low pay, rough conditions, misrepresentation in the media, and accusations that this education group is subversive and is paving the way for violence. Nevertheless, after eight months when they see the raised level of consciousness of the young people, their ability to read and write, their love for the Earth, and their willingness to support their parents in winning their rights, the joy stirring in the team is beyond words. No one can take it away and no slander can undo it.

I recall Joana, a longtime resident of the favela of Catumbi, who was active in community movements. When she was interviewed by the local newspaper, they asked her if her life had been good, and she said spontaneously, "Yes it has been good for me. I have struggled a great deal, but I have had the great joy of being able to raise my children and give them a professional education." She paused for a moment, thought, and added, smiling, "I now describe the struggle as 'fun' [*engraçado*, "amusing" lit. "graced"]. Back then it was suffering."

This godly joy is not accidental. It is the fruit of the self-denying effort of many. It produces abundant life because it comes from a practice of solidarity among all, a practice loved and blessed by God.

✠

Lord, where there is sadness let me sow joy. Grant that my joy may arise out of sincere compassion for those who suffer, true solidarity with those who are wronged, and my own conversion to universal kinship. Amen.

Where there is darkness, let me sow light

Only those familiar with darkness can know the light. Then they realize that simply lighting a match can dispel all the surrounding darkness.

There are many forms of darkness. Darkness of the *eyes*, or physical blindness, is one of the injuries most harmful to human beings. It robs the world of colors, landscapes, and human faces. When science restores the ability to see and brings light to the eyes of the blind, it is performing the messianic work of freeing from darkness.

Darkness of the *senses* is the inability to feel with the heart. Modern science has extended the capacity of the senses in its effort to identify the constants of nature, including the human organism. But it has atomized reality into a thousand pieces and has created a specific discipline for each of them. One person knows only plants, and among them only tropical plants, and among them only medicinal tropical plants, and among them only those that are anti-cancer, and so forth. This is the case in all fields of knowledge. Scientists have lost their view of the whole, and end up blinded to the complexity of reality.

Of the many dimensions of reason, they have elevated one, the instrumental-analytic dimension. In serving to bring the world partly under control, technological reason has on one hand made possible the construction of a death machine able to wipe out the biosphere several times, while on the other hand creating penicillin and reaching the moon.

But this utilitarian type of reason has exacted a heavy price. It has brought about a kind of blindness, a real lobotomy of the human spirit, which has become insensitive to the message of the beauty and grandeur of the universe. It has blinded itself to the mystery of what is real, placing emotion, feeling, and gentleness under suspicion, on the grounds that they impede objective knowledge of reality.

The effect of this visual and intellectual split has been to separate science from religion, economics from politics, politics from ethics, and ethics from spirituality. The unity of human experience has been torn asunder. The result is an appalling lack of care for nature, for human beings in the fullness of all their dimensions, with myriads of people living at or below survival level under conditions that are an affront to human dignity. The growing gap between the rich and poor gives rise to less and less ethical indignation.

There is also blindness of the *spirit*, a blindness toward the spiritual dimension of reality. Human beings have become spiritually blind when they do not grasp the "other world" within this world. They have lost the delicacy of spirit which identifies the sacred thread that unifies and re-unifies, preventing the part from capturing the dynamic whole which is harmonious and full of meaning. This subtle thread that binds and reconnects [re-liga] all is the creative principle: it is God.

Spiritual blindness prevents us from attending to the inner voice, God speaking to our conscience. It prevents us from seeing the poor and the wronged as a challenge to solidarity—a manifestation, for Christians, of the crucified Christ himself crying out for resurrection. These spiritual darknesses give us the sensation that we are lost, that we do not know who we are, nor whom we are serving.

What does it mean to sow light where there is darkness? It means having a generative attitude, one imbued with kindness and compassion, able to cast a different light on open wounds. Sometimes it entails the life-witness of someone who has suffered a great deal, whose suffering has not been in vain, because it has been refined, has matured, and has pointed the way to a new route toward life.

Finally, sowing light where there is darkness can mean introducing a living experience of the sacred, a word of wisdom from the spiritual masters of East and West, an inspired text of the Christian scriptures that can transmit an experience of light that reshapes the meaning of life and recreates the promise of blessed eternity. Is not this the witness of so many converts of yesterday and today?

Lord where there is darkness, may I bring light. You are the true light that enlightens every person who comes into this world. Enable me through inspired words, consoling gestures, and a warm heart to dissipate human darkness so that your light may show us the way and bring joy to life. Amen.

O Master

A master is more than a teacher, a doctor, or a technical expert. "Master" means a person who has reached such a degree of perfection that his or her technique has become art, and that he or she has become a master—whether in speaking, writing, painting, healing, playing soccer, counseling, or consoling.

Masters do more than teach—they live what they teach. Their lives witness to their ideas. Hence, the founders and most outstanding representatives of the spiritual traditions of Christianity, Buddhism, Hinduism, and other religious groups are called "masters." These traditions remain alive because they can produce other masters who energize followers, their disciples.

In the gospels Jesus is very often called Master and in the Christian tradition he is invoked as Divine Master. He takes his place not only in the tradition of masters of his people, but also in the great tradition of masters of humankind. Yet his greatness does not diminish the others, but enhances them by extending their mission and deepening their teachings. The New Testament writers called

Jesus "the Master" (cf. Mt 23:10) because they saw in him exceptional consistency and identification between what he taught and what he lived personally. In Christian usage, only God can be Master!

In contemporary terms, we could say that Jesus, like other masters of known religions, has become the archetypal Master. In him there is so much excellence of teaching, so much coherence between what he says and what he lives, so much light shining forth, that he becomes an exemplary figure and a universal reference point.

An archetype is never something inert. It is always linked to deep experiences of value and fullness of meaning. Encountering the archetype-Jesus means entering into a living dialogue with him from deep within ourselves, where he manifests himself as Master. It means listening to his message which becomes contemporary when confronted with issues that we live personally or that break in from the reality around us. It means placing ourselves at the feet of Jesus, as did his apostles and his friends, the sisters Martha and Mary.

With the Prayer for Peace we ask our inner Master—it can be Jesus or Mary, just as it can be Buddha, Krishna, Gandhi, Martin Luther King, the Dalai Lama, or other men and women—to teach us to practice all that we pray for here: that we may sow love, faith, truth, hope, joy, and light. Such are the values that produce peace and make us instruments of divine peace.

We likewise pray to the Master to bring us into the newness of his message, summed up in a short but great expression, *not so much . . . as to:* "*not so much* seek to be consoled, *as to* console; to be understood, *as to* understand; to be loved, *as to* love."

This "not so much . . . as to" expresses the inexhaustible flood of generosity found in the practice of Jesus and that of so many of his followers in history, such as Saint Francis of Assisi and Saint Clare, Leo Tolstoy and Archbishop Helder Camara, Mother Teresa, and so many other men and women. Because of this "not so much . . . as to," Jesus could love us and deliver himself for us when we were his enemies (Rom 5:8). Because of this "not so much . . . as to" he asks us to forget ourselves disinterestedly, to overcome ourselves, and to love without limits even those who perse-cute and slander us (Mt 5:10-11). That can happen only if, as in the Prayer of Saint Francis, we situate ourselves not as the *I* but as the *other*, seeking not *our* personal satisfaction, but the satisfaction of the *other*, not *our* salvation, but the salvation of the *other* and of the world.

When we recognize this "not so much . . . as to" in a person, we can calmly say: here is a true follower of the inner Master. This "not so much . . . as to" makes Jesus for-ever a Master, Master of the new age and divine Master.

O Master, make your wisdom and the example of your consis-tency to death resound within us. May we be your faithful dis-ciples by doing what you teach so that we may be truly instru-ments of love and peace. Amen.

Grant that I may not so much seek to be consoled as to console

At birth human beings are complete, but not yet ready. They are still on their way, and hence they are vulnerable. To survive and develop they have to work and create culture. In bodily terms, they need food and water; psychologically, they must feel accepted in family and community. Spiritually, they need to identify a fulfilling Meaning to transfigure their anxieties and illuminate the mystery of life and death.

Millions and millions live unprotected. They die prematurely of hunger and of a thousand illnesses, with no one to look after them. Millions and millions of others feel excluded from the human family, held to be of no account, expendable, dead weight in history. The market ignores whole countries which, because they are seen as having nothing to contribute to the world capitalist economy, are disregarded in any planning for health care, housing, education, and security.

How many young people are wandering directionless out there, hooked on drugs, cast out, left alone in their despair? Who will care for the elderly, the sick, the lonely, the physically and mentally handicapped, and those with HIV?

Sometimes collective distress affects whole peoples who are victims of ethnocide, as happened in the past with the Aztecs and Mayans, and is happening today with the Uaimiri-Astroaris in the Amazon. An eloquent witness to this distress is the elegy of an anonymous Quichua written in the sixteenth century in homage to the Inca Atahualpa, murdered by men under Francisco Pizarro, who devastated Peru: "Under a strange empire, we are overwhelmed with martyrdom, and we are destroyed, perplexed, lost, our memory denied, and alone; the protective shade dead, we weep with no one to turn to and nowhere to go; we are out of our minds; our wandering life scattered, surrounded by countless dangers, surrendered to alien hands." Who will console them, still scattered today?

There is the human, anonymous, everyday disconsolation, when people are faced with the irreparable loss of someone beloved, health, social status, a job. Who will console all of these people?

There is our total helplessness when we realize our powerlessness, when we cannot bring back a loved one who because of a stupid and avoidable accident, has departed in the prime of life—left for good. How relevant are the words of scripture now:

> "A voice was heard in Ramah,
> wailing and loud lamentation,

Rachel weeping for her children;
she would not be consoled, because they are no
    more." (cf. Mt 2:18)

In our great sadness, we yearn for gestures and words of consolation that will secure life that dissipates like water running through our fingers. How precious are those persons who approach with a mother's tenderness and a father's affection, give us a firm hug, wipe away our tears, and end our sobbing.

With good reason the prophets called on other prophets and priests in God's name, urging: "Console my people, console" (cf. Is 40:1; 49:13). One of the main functions of religion is to present the prospect of consolation in the face of the inexplicable dramas of life. It offers faith, according to which nothing is beyond God and everything is mysteriously part of his design of love for history and for the destiny of each person. Each one is called by the name known only to God and embraced with infinite tenderness.

Thus, we listen to the Master who asks us to be courageous, to have a stance like that of Abraham, so as to leave our own disconsolation behind and to go out to meet whoever has greater need of consolation. He invites us to surmount our own helplessness and to pay attention to the affliction of the one suffering, weeping, and sobbing nearby. Consoling rather than being consoled reveals the greatness of the human being. It is like Jesus on the cross, who forgot about his own wounds and heard the lament of the thief to whom he promised eternal life. And, at the end of history—as we are told in Revelation—God will intervene and

> "he will wipe every tear from their eyes.
> Death will be no more;
> mourning and crying and pain will be no more,
> for the old order has passed away." (cf. Rev 21:4)

Can any consolation be greater?

O Master, grant that I may seek not so much to be consoled as to console. May I be able to emerge from my own pain to hear the cry of the one suffering beside me. May I have words to console and gestures to create serenity, confident surrender, and profound peace. Amen.

Grant that I may not so much seek to be understood as to understand

One of the desires of human beings is to be able to be understood in what they think, propose, and do. How often we hear young people say, "No one understands me, no one loves me"? In family and interpersonal communications, words are often misunderstood, intentions are distorted and proposals are ridiculed. These things wound people internally and make them unwilling to share with others.

There are three basic ways to react to misunderstanding:

- To be open to dialogue, striving to clarify one's viewpoint, presenting the reasoning behind one's intentions.

- To close in on oneself, cutting off communication with people who are nearby and hardening oneself in one's own convictions.

- To strengthen one's own internal freedom and personal autonomy by building up a self-understanding that is independent of what other persons think or do not think, regardless of whether they are willing to dialogue or not.

The first approach, that of dialogue, is fruitful because every exchange is enriching. It can show our deficiencies, reveal our shadow dimension (which is always hard to acknowledge and integrate), and open up perspectives hidden from our own gaze. Every dialogue sheds light: it corrects mistakes and highlights what is most important. If we withdraw from exchange, how are we going to know what others think about the situation and about us? How are we going to know ourselves better? Do we not know ourselves better when we see ourselves from the standpoint of someone else who has a different (and perhaps better) reading of us?

In constructing our identity and preserving our self-esteem, which is necessary for balanced development, it is crucial that our intentions be understood and accepted. Few things wound us more than the distortion of our most cherished convictions.

The second approach, that of isolation, represents a flight to avoid confrontation. The result is that we lose the chance to grow because we encounter no resistance, and we deprive ourselves of the opportunity to clarify our thinking in the light of others' thoughts. This attitude can degenerate into arrogance and haughty contempt for others. When interactions are cut off, no living organism survives; it languishes and dies. The same thing happens with a human being who becomes isolated. No one is an island, for we are all enmeshed in networks of connections that nourish us and enable us to confront one another and grow.

The third approach, personal autonomy, represents an important aspect of the individuation process. A person grows not simply outward, in dialogue with others, or simply upward, by opening up to God and to ambitious dreams for humankind. Personal growth is most particularly inward, toward listening to the wisdom of the great elder who lives in the heart of each of us and who counsels and guides us in our human adventure. Building one's inner freedom certainly includes dialogue with others and with the surrounding reality. But it can also unfold when this dialogue is hindered and even cut off. Persons need to gradually free themselves from bitterness and dependencies so as to develop confidence in themselves and their potential.

We all have the right to be understood and so to be welcomed into human, personal, and social shared life, growing and fostering growth.

What does it mean to seek not so much to be understood as to understand? It is the experience of overcoming self in the direction of the other. Human beings seek not only the fullness of their being and their own potential—

that could mean narcissism. They are called to ever surpass themselves, an endeavor that is infinite and inexhaustible, finding rest only in God.

One succeeds in understanding more than being understood only when one radically loves the other, and for the other's sake displaces one's own center in order to rotate around the other's center. Faced with misunderstanding and even the distortion of one's own most cherished convictions, one strives to maintain dialogue, seeking to understand, accept, and pardon one's neighbor. This stance includes everyone, and embraces others for their own sake and as they actually are, not as one would have them be. One strives to accept and support the other, even when he or she makes mistakes and errors. Understanding in this manner is marvelous. Understanding is then perfect and complete. It is the divine within us.

✠

O Master, may I seek not so much to be understood as to understand. Grant that I may welcome others as they are. Only thus will I understand as I am understood. Grant that I may see the smallest sign of truth, goodness, and love in the other in order to strengthen it and enable it to come fully into the light. Amen.

Grant that I may not so much seek to be loved as to love

It is more gratifying to feel loved than to love, because one need only accept another's freely given love and need not win it or offer that person proofs of love.

To feel loved is to feel important and precious to someone. All at once, I know I am in the heart and mind of the other person; to that person I am priceless. That person is with me in every gesture, seeks to know every detail of my life story, prizes every word of mine, and lovingly intuits every intention, no matter how hidden it is.

A person in love lives in an altered state of consciousness, loses interest in himself or herself, and surrenders to forces pulling irresistibly toward the beloved, who in the lover's eyes is unique and different from everyone else in the universe. One experiences a state of ravishment and a surge of feeling that reorganizes one's whole life around the beloved.

We all want to be loved—everyone wants to be unique for someone. The saddest expression I ever heard came from a young social worker, with no particular endowments

of beauty according to the poor conventions of our material culture: "I've never been loved; I've never been interesting to anyone; to this day, no one has looked at me." Her
gaze was one of infinite sadness. A deep bitterness at the
bleakness and cruelty of life could be felt in her every word.
The universe seemed to have collapsed on her.

Without love, life loses meaning and intensity. Everything seems trivial and worthless. It is fundamental to the
brilliance of life that we feel loved and welcomed with affection by those around us. Perhaps behind atheism, ag-
nosticism, and indifference lies this devastating experience: the inability to sense a womb-like acceptance, being
embraced as within a family, and loved unconditionally by
another person.

Why do we have this inexpressible need to be loved?
Because from birth we human beings display the tendency
of wanting to be united to something that fulfills and tran-
scends us. The earth sciences tell us that this tendency
represents the action of the arrow of time and of the im-
pulse of evolution ever impelling us forward and upward
from convergence to convergence, toward a supreme culmination. Experts in the human psyche venture the idea
that this desire for union represents the ageless memory of
our life in our mother's womb. Religions teach that the
yearning is a longing for God as Alpha and Omega of our
life. Whatever it is, when human beings feel loved, they
have the experience that they have won back the earthly
paradise or have arrived at the promised land.

What does it mean to seek not so much to be loved as to love? It is the invitation to leap out of ourselves, so as to be able to foster love for the other and others. In loving the other, we want that person to have the experience of an absolute fulfillment—being loved—and to feel existentially like the emotional center of the universe. For that is exactly the experience that love makes possible.

Thus, loving more than being loved means having the strength to go out of ourselves so that we can be in the other for the sake of that other. Granting that other worth, care, tenderness, cordiality, and shared life, Saint Francis managed to love lepers and all creatures as his beloved brothers and sisters. That is why his universe is full of feeling, affection, and respect, because it enables all to feel loved.

This posture of a greater love can rescue threatened humankind and save the life of planet Earth. One who has this kind of abounding love has conquered all: his or her own heart, eternal salvation, and God.

✛

O Master, grant that I may seek not so much to be loved as to love. May I accept with generosity and joy the love that is granted to me, but may I strive particularly to make those around me feel loved. Grant that we may all feel loved by You so as to experience the supreme happiness granted in this life. Amen.

For it is in giving that we receive

The economy of spiritual goods is different from the economy of material goods. The more you give away material goods—money, land, houses, clothing, and food—the less you have. You become poorer and poorer until you end up in want. When very rich people spend lavishly and wastefully, they come to a miserable end.

The economy of spiritual goods is quite the reverse. The more we give, the more we receive; the more we surrender, the more we have. The more we love, show solidarity, spread good will, and practice forgiveness, the more we gain as human persons and the greater the esteem we receive. Spiritual goods are like love: they multiply by dividing; like fire, they increase by spreading.

We can understand this paradox if we consider the nature of human beings, who are beings of communication, as nodes of unlimited relationship. The more they go out of themselves and communicate with others, with nature, with different situations, and with God, the greater their chances of being enriched in knowledge, experience, and values. The more they go out to meet the other in dialogue, acceptance, and giving, the more they feel fulfilled in their essential personal core.

Hence, it is in giving that we receive. And countless times we receive more than we give. Is not this the experience that so many have when they devote themselves fully to others, when they accompany the poor and marginalized in solidarity, sharing in the process of forming a community on the outskirts of the city, a mothers' club, or a social organization? Going along with others, sharing their struggle for life, offering our skills, giving our time, offering a little of our ability to understand and love, all this produces a startling spiritual effect: we feel humanized and we go away enriched.

Even when people give away material goods within the context of the economy of spiritual goods (e.g., a person generously giving medical assistance or materially aiding very needy people as an expression of solidarity), they end up feeling that they are receiving more than they are giving. They experience the pleasing spiritual satisfaction of helping someone else. They know in their own lives the truth of what Saint Paul said to Christians in Miletus: "It is more blessed to give than to receive" (Acts 20:35).

Unfortunately, this notion from the Prayer of Saint Francis—"It is in giving that we receive"—is often cited to justify acts of selfishness and dishonesty: by supporting a particular government policy, a politician receives a benefit in return, even perhaps a significant sum of money. Justifying this unseemly practice with the expression, "It is in giving that we receive" entails a crude manipulation of the generous and unselfish spirit of Saint Francis and the gospel. The gospel precept is clear: "You received without cost, give without cost" (Mt 10:8); let one who gives do so without constraint and ulterior motives, "for God loves a cheerful giver" (2 Cor 9:7). One who gives magnanimously and with a sense of self-denial always receives in return, for nature is wise and generous and returns with great abundance. "The one who sows sparingly will also reap sparingly, and the one who sows bountifully will also reap bountifully" (2 Cor 9:6).

Thus, giving and receiving are intimately connected. This connection represents the basic logic that governs the operation of the universe and of nature itself. Everything is structured in a most intricate network of relationships, where all exist in one another, giving and receiving mutually what they need to live and develop within a subtle dynamic balance.

What matters is giving, and giving again. Only thus do we receive always and uninterruptedly goodness, love, grace, and life in abundance.

O Master, grant that we may understand that by giving generously and freely we will also receive all that we need in abundance. May we guide our lives by the generosity that will ever return to us more understanding, more acceptance, and more love. Amen.

It is in pardoning that we are pardoned

One of the most surprising and even scandalous dimensions of the message of Jesus is the proclamation that his God is a God of unconditional love and unlimited mercy. He offers his love and forgiveness to all, even when that love is not returned. He loves even the "ungrateful and evil" (Lk 6:35).

Such good news left the pious of his own time puzzled and still causes confusion today among people who strive to obey the commandments and make themselves pleasing to God. How can God also love the impious, sinners, exploiters, and evildoers? This is the paradox of Jesus' revolutionary message: God goes after the sheep that has gone astray and searches for the lost coin, runs out to meet the prodigal son and rejoices more over the sinner who repents than over the ninety-nine just who are saved. Jesus says, "I have not come to call the just, but sinners" (Mk 2:17). How can we fail to be surprised at such words?

Curiously, all of Jesus' parables about forgiveness and mercy are aimed at the hardness of heart of pious persons of his time. The parables of the Pharisee and the publican (Lk 18:9-14) and the prodigal son (Lk 15:11-32) seek to show that in order to please God, besides being faithful and good, we must also be merciful and wish to forgive, to forgive "seventy times seven" (Mt 18:22), that is, without limit. We must seek "to be merciful just as your Father is merciful" (Lk 6:36).

If God forgives us so unreservedly, how can we not also forgive those who offend us? The gospel is emphatic: "For if you forgive others their transgressions, your heavenly Father will also forgive you; but if you do not forgive others, neither will your Father forgive your transgressions" (Mt 6:14-15). Is this some kind of negotiation with God? No. It has to do with understanding that "the measure with which you measure will be measured out to you" (Mt 7:2). According to the parable, the indebted servant was completely forgiven for the thousands of denarii that he owed, but he did not forgive his fellow servant who owed him a few coins. The master called him and told him, "You wicked slave! I forgave you all that debt because you pleaded with me. Should you not have had mercy on your fellow slave, as I had mercy on you?" (Mt 18:32-33). The lesson is crystal clear: "Just as the Lord has forgiven you, so you also must forgive" (Col 3:13).

This attitude is not easy for those whose sense of justice is merely human. Do not many say "I'd rather die than forgive"? We must live the experience of being radically forgiven in our offenses to feel impelled to forgive without reservations and with a free heart.

At the culmination of history, works of mercy will count. They will enable the supreme and merciful Judge to announce: "Come, you who are blessed by my Father, inherit the kingdom prepared for you from the foundation of the world" (Mt 25:34).

What does it mean existentially to forgive? It means seeking to go beyond oneself, leaving bitterness and the will to vengeance behind, and reaching a higher level from which we will be able to see differently the one who has done injury. Such people are not simply people who have done wrong. They are an infinite openness, children of God, and brothers and sisters in our shared humanity. Hence, they cannot be reduced to simply being "offenders" and "sinners." Forgiving means preventing them from being held hostage to the consequences of the wrongful acts they have committed. Forgiving means the ability to support and maintain the bond of communion even when the other side is closed and the other margin disappears. It means allowing love to flow once more. Wagering on this positive side means creating through forgiveness the conditions for a relationship of shared life in kinship.

✚

O Master, often and in many ways you have forgiven us unreservedly, as a loving Mother forgives a child. Grant that we may also forgive those who have wronged us, and that we will never cease believing in generosity of heart, which can forgive even when unjustly wounded by many offenses. Amen.

And it is in dying that we are born to eternal life

Death can be understood in many ways. The most common, as well as the poorest, understands death as a mere biological phenomenon, the separation of body and soul, the conclusion of the earthly course of the human adventure.

Today life is increasingly understood as the self-organization of matter, matter which is never inert, but rather a very sophisticated complex of interactions. Life, from the most basic amoeba to us, is one and sacred in its many manifestations. It goes through many passages and ever higher and more cooperative levels of realization. Death is part of life, and represents the process of transformation and passage from one level of life to another.

We understand that death belongs to life if it we see it as part of the basic structure of our own life. What is that structure? It is rootedness and openness. Each of us is rooted in an existential arrangement with a heavy bio-psycho-social load. This is the actual world, with possibilities limited by family, profession, cultural level, and the state of consciousness proper to each one. This is rootedness.

At the same time, human beings are open to the world around them: they interact with it, exchange information, and make personal syntheses that shape their history. This is openness.

Life is a difficult interplay between rootedness and opening. If people close in on their rootedness, at the expense of opening, they feel stifled and do not grow. If they open up and forget their roots, they become alienated and lose identity.

In order to adequately connect rootedness and opening, a human being must incorporate death. Death nullifies certain arrangements, makes others possible, and brings about changes that open new chances for life. For example: I love my family a great deal (rootedness). But the time comes when I have to pull myself away from it (opening). I have to die to my family; otherwise, I will not make my own way through the world and I do not create my own family. After dying to my family, I arise to a new relationship with it. Another example: sexual intimacy is important in a couple's relationship (rootedness). But it can mean obsessive attachment that is harmful to both sides. It has to die to this unbalanced form in order to rise to a new loving relationship (openness) which enriches intimacy without being held hostage to it. The death in these examples is a liberation, the necessary passage toward a higher and more complex level of life. As is evident, death does not come from the outside; it is built into the very fabric of life.

Human beings are not simply open to some things; they are absolute openness. Their structure of desire arouses an insatiable thirst for essential being to which they wish to be united by feeling, understanding, and love. They do not rest as long as they do not see it unveiled and veiled behind everything and within each being. Any encounter with it produces joy and at the same time increases the yearning to experience it and be with it. The universe in its immeasurable vastness, time in its already billions of years of duration, and life in its unimaginable complexity cannot replace essential Being. They are particular and limited manifestations of it. They are always part and parcel of the Whole which is unattainable as Whole.

What is the purpose of death? It allows desire to reach supreme fulfillment. With death a break with space-time limitation (rootedness) takes place, thereby creating the possibility of a leap (openness) into essential Being. We arise to a new kind of life and presence in the universe on the basis of our insertion into essential Being.

Death is an intelligent invention of life to make possible the realization of its basic purpose: that of union with essential Being, of sharing eternally with it.

Thus, death is gain. Remaining in the kind of life that is now ours means never being able to grow fully, be transformed, and be able to rise. It means never being able to plunge into the originating Fount of all being. Saint Francis rightly said: "It is in dying that we are born to eternal life." It is in dying that we rise, and live more and better. He intuits this truth so well that, as he is dying, he calls death "Sister" and invites her to open the gates of Supreme Life for him. That is why he can die singing.

✠

O *Master, teach us to live in such a way that we welcome death as friend and sister. It does not take away life, but leads to the Fount of all life. Grant that we may be able to recognize in earthly life the beginnings of celestial and eternal life.* Amen.

Bibliography

Armstrong, Regis, ed. *Francis and Clare: The Complete Works.* Ramsey, N.J: Paulist Press, 1982.

———, et al., eds. *Francis of Assisi: Early Documents.* 3 vols. New York: New City Press, 1999–.

Balducci, E. *Francesco d'Assisi.* Florence: Edizioni Cultura della Pace, 1989.

Blofield, J. *A deusa da compaixão e do amor.* São Paulo: IBRASA, 1995.

Boff, L. *Saint Francis.* New York: Crossroad, 1984.

Doyle, E. *Francisco de Assis e o Cântico da Fraternidade Universal.* São Paulo: Paulinas, 1985.

Esser, K. *Temi Spirituali.* Milan: Edizioni Biblioteca Francescana, 1973.

———. *Studien zu den Opuscula des hl. Franziskus von Assis. Historisches Institut der Kapuziner,* 276 ff., note 53. Rome: Grottaferrata, 1973.

Herrigel, E. *Zen in the Art of Archery.* New York: Random House, 1999.

———. *The Method of Zen.* New York: Random House, 1974.

Iriarte, L. *Vocação Franciscana.* Petrópolis: Vozes, 1977.

König, F. *Die Friedensgebete von Assisi.* Freiburg: Herder, 1987.

Leclerc, E. *The Canticle of Creatures: Symbols of Union.* Chicago: Franciscan Herald Press, 1977.

Manselli, R. *St. Francis of Assisi.* Chicago: Franciscan Herald Press, 1988.

Merton, T. *The Way of Chuang Tzu.* New York: New Directions, 1965.

Nerburn, K. *Make Me an Instrument of Your Peace. Living in the Spirit of the Prayer of Saint Francis.* San Francisco: Harper San Francisco, 1998.

Nhat Hanh, Thich. *Being Peace.* Berkeley: Parallax Press, 1987.

Silveira, I. *São Francisco de Assis e a "Nossa irmã e mãe Terra."* Petrópolis: Vozes, 1994.

Short, William. *Poverty and Joy: The Franciscan Tradition.* Maryknoll, N.Y.: Orbis Books, 1999.

Sticco, M. *São Francisco de Assis.* Petrópolis: Vozes, 1984.

Surian, C. *Dinâmica do Desejo: Freud, Cristo, Francisco de Assis.* Petrópolis: Vozes, 1982.